Peter and Paul
in the Church of Rome

Theological Inquiries

Studies in Contemporary
Biblical and Theological Problems

General Editor
Lawrence Boadt, C. S. P.

PAULIST PRESS
New York • Mahwah

Peter and Paul
in the Church of Rome

The Ecumenical Potential
of a Forgotten Perspective

William R. Farmer

Roch Kereszty

PAULIST PRESS
New York ● Mahwah

Acknowledgement
Chapter Four was originally published in a somewhat different form in COM-MUNIO 14 (1988): 215–33.

Library of Congress Cataloging-in-Publication Data

Farmer, William Reuben.
    Peter and Paul in the church of Rome : the ecumenical potential of
a forgotten perspective / William R. Farmer, Roch Kereszty.
        p.   cm. — (Theological inquiries)
    Includes bibliographical references.
    ISBN 0-8091-3102-1
    1. Papacy and Christian union.   2. Peter, the Apostle, Saint.
3. Paul, the Apostle, Saint.   4. Popes—Primacy.   5. Catholic
Church—Doctrines.   6. Protestant churches—Doctrines.
I. Kereszty, Roch A.   II. Title.   III. Series.
BX9.5.P29F37   1989
262'.13—dc20   89-12838
                                                           CIP

Published by Paulist Press
997 Macarthur Boulevard
Mahwah, NJ 07430

Printed and bound in the
United States of America

CONTENTS

PREFACE by Robert Lee Williams   vii

1. THE ECUMENICAL POTENTIAL OF A
    FORGOTTEN PERSPECTIVE ON THE
    CHURCH OF ROME   1

2. NEW TESTAMENT FOUNDATIONS   12

3. PETER AND PAUL IN THE THEOLOGIES OF
    IRENAEUS AND TERTULLIAN   53

4. HISTORICAL SURVEY AND SYSTEMATIC
    REFLECTIONS   82

5. A RESPONSE TO CHAPTER 4 FROM A
    PROTESTANT PERSPECTIVE   98

6. FURTHER CONVERGENCE WITH
    CONTINUING DIFFERENCES OVER
    COLLEGIALITY   122

    EPILOGUE by Albert C. Outler   130

    NOTES   138

    INDICES   152

We dedicate this study
to the memory of
ALBERT C. OUTLER,
whose love for
the Una Sancta Catholica
has inspired our work.

Fr. Roch A. Kereszty, O. Cist., was born in Hungary in 1933, earned a graduate degree in library science from the University of Budapest in 1956, and the S.T.D. from the University of St. Anselm in Rome in 1963. His dissertation was entitled "Wisdom in the Spiritual Theology of St. Bernard." The same year he joined the Cistercian Monastery, Our Lady of Dallas, and began teaching systematic theology at the University of Dallas. While continuing to teach at the university, Fr. Kereszty became chairman of the theology department of the Cistercian Preparatory School in 1970, and novice master for the monastery in 1975. He serves as consulting editor for the international Catholic review, *Communio.* His publications include *God Seekers for a New Age* (Pflaum Press, 1970) and a textbook on christology for the Hungarian church (1977). He has written a number of articles on christology, ecclesiology, and spirituality for the *American Ecclesiastical Review, Communio,* and *The Second Century,* as well as for Belgian and Hungarian journals. Currently Fr. Kereszty is completing a work on christology for an English-speaking audience.

Professor William R. Farmer was born in 1921 and was educated at Occidental College (B.A.), Cambridge University (M.A.) and Union Theological Seminary (Th.D.). Since 1959 he has been on the faculty of Perkins School of Theology, Southern Methodist University, teaching courses in New Testament. Dr. Farmer has received numerous research grants and fellowships, including the Guggenheim Fellowship. In addition to contributing articles to journals and reference works, he is well-known for his studies on the Jewish background of the New Testament, the synoptic problem, and the canon. More recently, as co-chairman of the International Institute for Renewal of Gospel Studies, he has been involved in the 1984 International Conference on the Relationships of the Gospels in Jerusalem, and the Cambridge Conference on the Eucharistic Texts at St. Edmond's College in 1988. At present Professor Farmer is also serving as a co-director of the 1989 Conference on the Social History of Matthew under the auspices of the Center for the Study of Religion in the Greco-Roman World.

Professor Albert C. Outler, deemed "one of the pre-eminent Protestant ecumenists of our years" by Martin Marty in the *Christian Century* in 1984, was Professor of Theology emeritus at Perkins School of Theology, S.M.U. A patrologist by training, an ecumenist by choice, he taught at Duke and Yale before going to S.M.U. He lectured and published extensively in ecumenical church history and theology; he co-chaired the World Council of Churches' epoch-making study of "Tradition and Traditions" (1953–63). He was a delegated observer to the Second Vatican Council (1962–65) from the World Methodist Council. Three of his fourteen honorary degrees were from Roman Catholic universities and, in 1987, he received the *Pax Christi* Award from St. John's Abbey and University for "outstanding contributions to ecumenical understanding." Before his death, Professor Outler was in the process of completing a programmatic essay for the *Ecumenical Review* in preparation for worldwide discussion of the theme, "Come, Holy Spirit, Renew the Whole Creation," at the World Council of Churches meeting in Canberra in 1991.

Dr. Robert Lee Williams, editor of this volume, is the Patrick Henry, Jr., Post-Doctoral Research Fellow of the International Institute for Renewal of Gospel Studies. He completed a Ph.D. dissertation, "Bishop Lists: Episcopal Authority in Ecclesiastical Polemics," under Professor Robert M. Grant in the Department of New Testament and Early Christian Literature at the University of Chicago. His interests include the gospels and the social history of early Christianity, especially in relation to orthodoxy and heresy.

PREFACE

This contribution to ecumenical research arises from inter-action between Catholics and Protestants in the Seminar on the Development of Early Catholic Christianity, composed of faculty members from seminaries and universities in North Texas. Although ecumenical dialogue sometimes consists more in stating similarities and differences than in engaging one another on them, the spirit of this seminar has led these two scholars to engage in a more genuine dialogue. That spirit calls for a certain measure of mutuality, openness in the heart, and careful thinking. Nowhere is such treatment more needed than in concerns over the Catholic view of Peter and the Protestant view of Paul. Such dialogue offers hope for biblically "organic" unity in the faith. Professor Outler has appended eloquent ruminations on this glorious prospect. As a member of the seminar, I have appreciated the serious exploration of convergence and divergence of views by the authors. As a researcher in both New Testament and early Christian literature, I was happy to serve as editor of this volume. I particularly commend to my Protestant brothers and sisters of evangelical sympathies the form of ecumenical quest found herein. Professor Farmer and Father Kereszty hope that their investigation of the roles of Peter and Paul will encourage their readers to probe further for a greater understanding in the faith and will result in a more informed unity of the faith.

I wish to thank my wife, Patricia, for her assistance to me in the preparation of the indices.

Robert Lee Williams

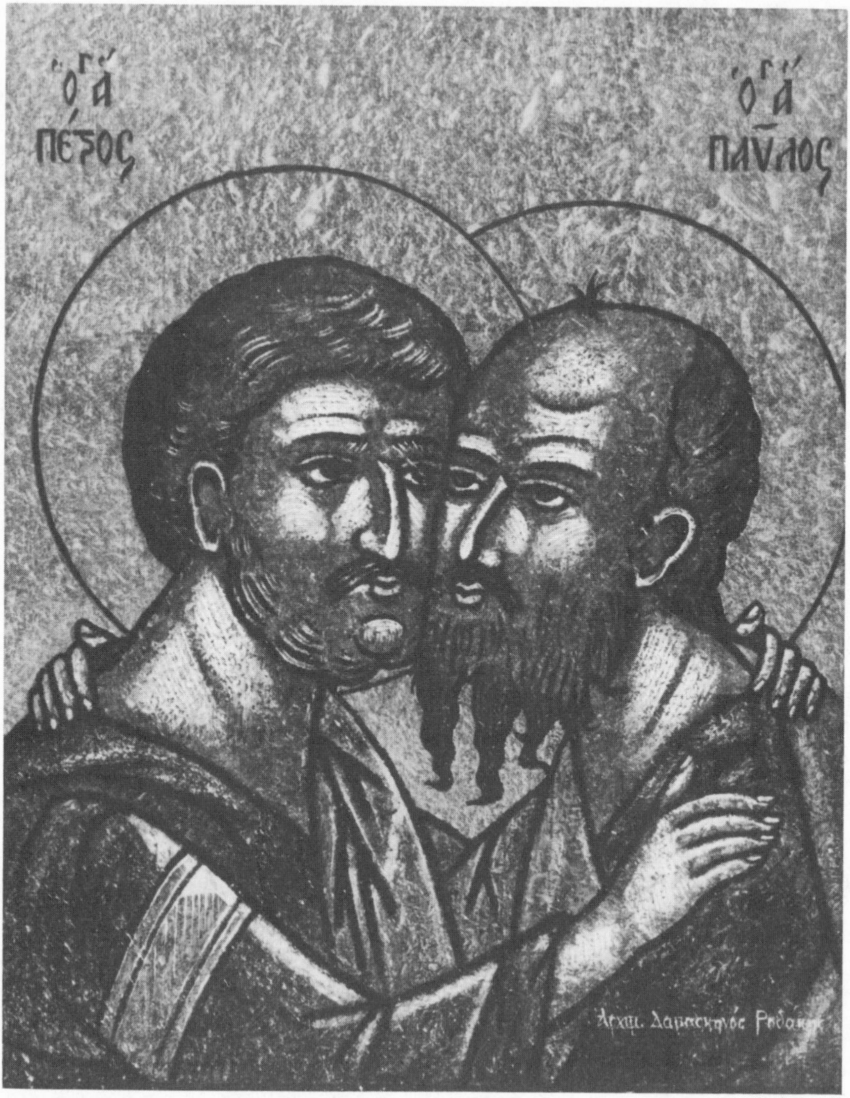

ΠΕΤΡΟΣ
ΠΑΥΛΟΣ
Αρχιμ. Δαμασκηνός

Chapter One

THE ECUMENICAL POTENTIAL OF A FORGOTTEN PERSPECTIVE ON THE CHURCH OF ROME

THE NEED FOR A BROADER PERSPECTIVE

Regarding the role of the church of Rome in the universal church, ecumenical research in America has concentrated on the single question of Peter: the origin, development and meaning of the Petrine traditions in the New Testament and the possible continuation of the Petrine ministry in the bishops of Rome.[1] While this line of work remains important, we believe it needs to be integrated in a larger perspective.

In the past decades European scholarship has rediscovered the joint role of Peter and Paul in the New Testament and in patristic literature. Yet historical and theological research is far from being completed and even the results already obtained have failed so far to make an impact on the ecumenical scene in America. Our study intends to build upon and continue the works of Congar, Tillard and Allmen and make the fruits thus obtained available for the ecumenical dialogue.[2] We intend to show that there is a broader perspective for the role of the church of Rome in the church universal, a perspective which is both more traditional and ecumenically more promising than that of the Petrine succession considered in isolation. Our study claims on the basis of biblical, liturgical, and patristic tradition, a tradition that has echoed in the official documents of the bishop of Rome up to the present, that the special role and authority of this church is based on the authority of the apostles Peter *and* Paul. This perspective

1

does not contradict the Roman Catholic dogma of the primacy of the bishop of Rome but is in some tension with its customary interpretation and provides a challenge to understand it better in a broader context.

The volume consists of this common document (Chapter 1) we have jointly authored, and of individual studies (Chapter 2– Chapter 5) we have developed in cooperation with each other. The common document outlines the points of convergence in our work while the results of our individual research are presented in the subsequent chapters. Chapter 2 (Farmer) treats some of the most important biblical foundations; Chapter 3 (Kereszty) the role of Peter and Paul as well as that of the church of Rome in the thought of the two most influential early theologians, Irenaeus and Tertullian. Chapter 4 (Kereszty) provides a brief historical survey up to the present and spells out the theological implications of the theme for Roman Catholic theology. Chapter 5 (Farmer) responds from a Protestant perspective to the previous chapter's Roman Catholic conclusions. In the last chapter again jointly authored we explore one important consequence of the joint Petrine-Pauline heritage for the bishop of Rome, namely the collegial nature of his authority. We can there identify more clearly than before the differences between our views but also spell out some further common ground.

It should be obvious that in this book we speak neither for the Methodist nor for the Roman Catholic church, but only for ourselves. As individual historians and theologians, we are testing the normally accepted limits of the Methodist and Roman Catholic theological positions in search for a consensus. The limited and provisional consensus that we have reached intends to remain faithful to the principles of our respective traditions.

PRESUPPOSITIONS AND METHOD

The Roman Catholic church considers it part of divine revelation that the bishop of Rome is the successor of the apostle Peter in a special way and on this basis the pope has supreme universal and immediate jurisdiction over the universal church and shares in the infallibility of the universal church when he defines its faith *ex cathedra*. At the same time, however, the Roman Catholic tradition does not hold any dogmatic statement for an unsurpassable and full formulation of a revealed truth, but acknowledges its imperfect character. Every defined dogma is open to and even calls for further deepening of understanding and for a further reintegrating of the dogma into the totality of the Christian mystery. It also happens quite often—a necessary consequence of the nature of human understanding—that a new and more precise articulation of one truth of faith occasions an eclipsing or at least an obscuring of other elements of revelation. Hence, the need in Roman Catholic theology to return constantly to the sources of God's revelation, in particular to the scriptures and to the patristic and liturgical tradition, in order to recover what has been, to a greater or lesser degree, forgotten. Less bound by official dogma, Protestants, at least in theory, are even freer to return constantly to the sources in order to be judged, renewed and replenished by them. For Protestants, these sources mean, in a special way, the scriptures. Meanwhile, one of the most positive fruits of Vatican II has been the growing recognition, on the Catholic side, that the whole preaching and the whole life of the church must be ruled by scripture. At the same time, on the Protestant side, there is now an awareness that the church's tradition may be an important key in understanding the scriptures. In this process of "resourcement" we believe that the studying of the life and beliefs of the great church in the second century is of decisive importance. This is the church that Protestants, Roman Catholics, and Orthodox acknowledge as constituting their common ancestry. This is the church that selected those writings which would constitute the New Testament canon of scriptures for all Christian churches that exist today. These writings came from a wide range of "apostolic" literature representing various trends in the nascent church and in their complementarity and apparent contradictions presented the church of the second century with an ecumenical task of extraordinary magnitude. Christians of all confessions, in accepting today the scripture canon as binding, thereby accept implicitly the insight and the judgement of the second century church which recognized the apostolic witness in these sometimes diverging yet predominantly converging writings. Acknowledging as normative this judgment of the second century church on the scripture canon prompted us to investigate her belief on the importance of the role which the joint martyrdom of Peter and Paul in Rome has played in the history of the Catholic church and the development of her New Testament canon.

THE AGREEMENT OF PETER AND PAUL AND THEIR JOINT FOUNDATION OF THE CHURCH OF ROME THROUGH TEACHING AND MARTYRDOM[3]

For Irenaeus, Tertullian and Origen the doctrinal agreement of Peter and Paul is crucially important in refuting all the heretics. Peter and Paul together embody the apostolic witness and stand for all the other apostles even though their testimony is complemented by that of James and John.

According to the earliest available evidence (Clement of Rome, Ignatius of Antioch, Dionysius of Corinth, Irenaeus and Tertullian) Peter and Paul together founded the church of Rome. Peter is not the first bishop of Rome according to the earliest succession list in the *Against Heresies* of Irenaeus. Both Peter and Paul hand over the ministry of the episcopate to Linus after they founded and built up the church (3.3.3). Only in the third century does Peter appear as the first bishop of Rome. Yet as late as the fourth century the synod of Arles attributes the prominence of Rome to the fact that the apostles Peter and Paul sit in judgment in that city. While in the patristic age the bishops of Rome refer to Peter as the one who carries on his ministry through them, yet they prefer to describe this ministry by a Pauline phrase: the blessed Peter carries in them the "sollicitudo omnium ecclesiarum" (2 Cor 11:28). Even the standard phrase "let him be anathema" expressing the excommunication of a heretic in the decrees of the Roman magisterium (as well as in conciliar decrees) is a typical Pauline phrase (Gal 1:8,9; cf. also 1 Cor 12:3; 16:22).

The liturgy preserves up to this day the awareness that both Peter and Paul are patrons of the church of Rome and that the pope relies on the authority of both. The liturgical prayers throughout the history of the church center attention not so much on the bishop of Rome as the successor of Peter and Paul as on the belief that, through their prayers, Peter and Paul together protect, strengthen, and rule the church of Rome and thereby fulfill their mission for the universal church. Their apostolic task did not end with their martyrdom. On the contrary, the day of martyrdom is their birth day. It is through their martyrdom that they become perfected as apostles: their very existence is taken up and transformed into the act of witnessing to Christ. Through their new life in Christ they become "free men" (cf. Ignatius, Rom IV.3) so that they can carry out their apostolic mission in the church of Rome without any time limitation. As long as the principality of the church of Rome remains based on the martyr witness of her two founding apostles, both Peter and Paul are seen to found this principality. The second century church follows the lead of the New Testament writers (Mt 18:16; 2 Cor 13:1; Jn 8:19; 1 Tim 5:19) in transforming the legal requirement of the Old Testament (Dt 19:15) into a theological principle: the teachings of Christ must be witnessed to by the agreement of two or three witnesses.

In summary, we can state the rationale for the normative role of Rome in the early church: it was founded by the two apostles Peter and Paul whose joint martyrdom sealed their joint witnessing. This is the reason for the famous statement of Irenaeus that will be attested unanimously for centuries (even though understood in a different context) by both the western and eastern church:

> every church, i.e. the faithful from everywhere, must be in harmony with this church because of its most excellent origin; in which (church) the tradition coming from the apostles has always been preserved for the faithful from everywhere (*Ag Her* 3.3.2.).

New Testament Foundations

Is the patristic view on the normative character of the joint martyrdom of Peter and Paul for the church of Rome attested in the New Testament? Since their death in Rome preceded the for-

mation of the New Testament canon, and indeed the composition of many of the books of the New Testament, it should not
surprise us to find the importance of their basic theological agreement, their joint witnessing, and their martyrdom reflected in the
various documents of the New Testament and in the structure of
its canon.

The Joint Role of Peter and Paul

Galatians tells us that, three years after his conversion, Paul
spent fifteen days with Peter "in order to visit with him" (1:18).
Up to now, the importance of this visit had been, by and large,
overlooked by biblical scholarship. Paul's concern for the truth
of the traditions he had received from the church of Peter and
the length of the visit make it hardly possible to view it as a mere
courtesy call or a get-acquainted visit. It is most likely that Paul
questioned at length the chief eyewitness of the earthly life of
Jesus and the first witness of the risen Christ about those
traditions whose truth Paul considered central to his preaching.
The traditions which he most likely discussed with Peter include
the atoning death and resurrection of Christ as fulfilling the scripture, in particular Isaiah 53, the Lord's supper and the appearances of the risen Lord. He must have clarified with Peter that
the appearance he received had been of the same order as the
appearance to Peter and to the other apostles (cf. 1 Cor 15:1–7
and 1 Cor 11:23–26).

Fourteen years later Paul goes up again to Jerusalem to settle
the controversy which was aroused by the fact that he and Barnabas admitted the Gentiles into the church without subjecting
them to the law of Moses. Those "who seemed to be pillars,"
James, Peter and John, agree with Paul's teaching and practice
and extend a handshake of fellowship to him and Barnabas. They
acknowledge that Paul has received the "grace" of an apostolic
mission to the Gentiles from the same God who has given an
apostolic mission to Peter among the circumcised (Gal 2:1–10).

This handshake of *koinōnia,* in particular, the agreement of
Peter and Paul, is embodied and reflected in the composition of
the New Testament canon. Most writings of the New Testament

are linked, in some way, to one of the four participants of the Jerusalem meeting, but in a special way to Peter and Paul. The synoptic gospels present Peter as the chief eyewitness guarantor of the tradition concerning the public ministry, death and resurrection of Jesus and the leader of the twelve. (The fourth gospel is accepted into the canon only with the appendix that affirms the role of Peter as chief shepherd.) The second half of the canon is dominated by the Pauline corpus. Yet these two halves of the canon mutually influenced each other. On the one hand, all the gospels seem to have undergone, to various degrees, some Pauline (or rather deutero-Pauline) influence. On the other hand, 1 and 2 Peter suggest a Petrine control over the Pauline churches and writings. 1 Peter attributes to Peter the Pauline literary genre of apostolic letter and addresses his letter to the Pauline churches. 2 Peter implies that it is Peter who holds the key to the right interpretation of the Pauline corpus (3:15).

In the middle of the canon stands Acts which in miniature reflects the composition of the canon itself: the first half of Acts is dominated by the figure of Peter, the second by Paul.

The Importance of Rome in God's Plan of Salvation

Paul's daring act of writing as he did to the Christians at Rome, a church he did not actually found, makes most sense if we see it in relationship to the conference in Jerusalem where, with Peter's support, his mission to the Gentiles was recognized and approved by the other apostles in Jerusalem. In other words, Paul's letter to the Romans presupposes the fundamental Jerusalem agreement. This also entitles Paul to seek the help of the Roman Christians for supporting his mission to Spain.

According to Acts 23:11, as Paul witnessed to Jesus in Jerusalem so must he also witness to him in Rome. That Paul's *martyrēsai* in Rome will actually be his martyrdom in Rome can be surmised from reading Acts 23:11 in conjunction with Paul's sermon in Miletus (20:18–38, esp. vv 25, 38). That Paul's arrival and witnessing in Rome is the providential climax and consummation of his apostolic mission, as well as an important event in the life of the church, appears from the structure of Acts: his mission begins in Jerusalem and concludes with a preaching ministry in Rome.

Although we do not know when Peter came to Rome, 1 Peter presents him as writing from Babylon (5:13). The name Babylon designates Rome as a world power hostile to God and persecuting God's people (cf. also Rev 14:8; 16:19; 17:5; 18:2). The fact that Peter writes from "Babylon" underlines the martyrological significance of the city of Rome. As the faith of the three young men endured the test of fire in the flaming furnace of the king of Babylon, so now is the faith of Christians being tested through trial and persecution—just as gold must pass through the assayer's fire (1 Pet 1:7; 4:12).

The Joint Martyrdom of the Apostles Peter and Paul as Constitutive of Their Apostolic Mission

The martyrdom of both apostles, adumbrated and anticipated in the New Testament, is not extrinsic to, but rather constitutive of their apostolic mission (cf. 1 Pet; 2 Tim 4:6, 16–18; Jn 21:18–19). If Matthew 16:17–19 is read in context it is evident that Peter will not be able to fulfill his role as the rock on which the church is to be built (and cannot hold the keys to the kingdom of heaven) unless he is ready to follow Jesus into martyrdom. As long as he persists in his stubborn refusal of the cross he is not a rock but a stumbling block, a mouthpiece for Satan and a hindrance to the fulfilling of God's plan (cf. Mt 16:21–24). Thus Peter's role as the leading apostle is conditioned on his acceptance of the cross. John 21:15–19 has a very similar message. If Peter is to continue the mission of Jesus as the good shepherd who lays down his life for his sheep he must follow Jesus by imitating his death. Peter's martyrdom, then, is the actual consummation of his "office" as representing the chief shepherd Jesus.

2 Timothy seems to be a *post eventum* portrait of the apostle-martyr Paul by one of his disciples. From a human viewpoint Paul's situation is pictured as totally desperate: everybody abandoned him at his first trial; his death seems imminent (4:16, 18). Nevertheless, in this hopeless situation the Lord empowered Paul that through him "the preaching (of the gospel) might be fulfilled

and all the nations might hear it" (4:17). This bold extension of Paul's influence to "all the nations" is more than rhetorical exaggeration. It becomes understandable from the theological connection between martyrdom and apostleship: the apostolic preaching of Paul is consummated, increased to universal dimensions, and perpetuated through his final act of witnessing. His preaching, in this final form, will indeed reach through time and space all the nations of the world.

However, in the light of Galatians 2:9, the fact that Peter and Paul suffered martyrdom together, in the same city of Rome, adds further weight to their testimony. They sealed with their blood their common witness to Jesus Christ and gave special meaning to that initial handshake of fellowship which liberated the Christian church for discharging its universal mission throughout the centuries.

CONSEQUENCES FOR SYSTEMATIC THEOLOGY

We hope that the insights we have gained from scripture and patristic theology will shed some new light on the Catholic dogma of Petrine primacy, and move the ecumenical discussion in a direction where agreement can more easily be reached.

That the prominence of the church of Rome, according to the New Testament and the earliest patristic tradition, derives from its foundation by both Peter and Paul must be taken seriously by systematic theology. Equally important for systematic theology is the early patristic evidence and the constant witness of the liturgy that the church of Rome is no less an heir to Paul than to Peter. In the light of these facts the mission of the bishop of Rome appears to consist in perpetuating through history the Jerusalem handshake of fellowship between Peter and Paul (and Barnabas, James and John), embodied in the New Testament canon and sealed in Rome with the blood of both apostles. In carrying out the ministry of Peter, he is the guardian against distortions and the harmonizer of the various trends of the Christian tradition. In fidelity to the mission of Paul, he is the missionary for the Gentiles, freeing the gospel from the cultural encumbrance of past ages and promoting its "incarnation" in new cultures—all of this, of course, not alone but collegially. Moreover, following the example of Paul, the bishop of Rome should encourage, test and coordinate all the various charisms in the church. In all these capacities, the bishop of Rome has the responsibility to be a model for every bishop and missionary of Jesus Christ.

Once we formulate the "job description" of the bishop of Rome in these Petrine and Pauline terms, we observe that, consciously or unconsciously, the popes in fact have quite often lived up to it in history. In the first centuries they formulated in Pauline terms the task which, according to their belief, Peter was carrying out through them. But even later, up to the present, they considered themselves as "a missionary to the nations." In fact, many of the major missionary thrusts of the western church (to England, to some of the Slavic nations, to Hungary, to Latin America, Africa and Asia) were initiated by Rome. The best bishops of Rome were also quite sensitive to charismatic movements, allowed them freedom and defended them from oppression and reprisals (e.g., the support of the Franciscans by Innocent III, and, most recently, Pope John XXIII liberating the forces of renewal by convoking Vatican II).

CONSEQUENCES FOR ECUMENICAL DIALOGUE

An awakening to the fact that the bishop of Rome is an heir to both Paul and Peter has important consequences for both Catholics and Protestants. Catholics will more easily understand the importance of the Pauline heritage and see more sympathetically the legitimate concerns of Protestants for whom Paul's understanding of the gospel was normative. If Protestants who view Paul's gospel as the implicit canon of the New Testament and themselves as the heirs and guardians of that canon see that the present church of Rome increasingly acknowledges and practices the heritage of Paul as well as that of Peter, they may more readily perceive in that church a living link to the apostolic witness of Peter and Paul embodied in the New Testament. Protestants and Roman Catholics (and it may eventually include the Orthodox as well) could then arrive at a common description of the role of the bishop of Rome in the following terms: *Within the divine economy of the one holy catholic church, the mission of the church of Rome consists in bearing witness to and living out of the united witness of the apostles Peter and Paul, and in reminding other churches which accept the New Testament canon of their obligation to do the same.* Even though every local church has this very same vocation and obligation, the church of Rome, by virtue of sacred history, is under divine constraint to remember the history of her foundation by the martyr apostles Peter and Paul and to bear witness for the faithful from everywhere to the truth of this apostolic faith.

This agreement still leaves many important questions unresolved. For instance, how could we further specify that common relationship of the bishop of Rome to Peter and Paul which we describe as the bishop of Rome being "no less an heir to Paul than to Peter"? What consequences can we draw from this common relationship? What does "reminding other churches of their obligation to live out of that united witness" actually entail? Does it include the charism for the bishop of Rome to teach the faith of the church with authority? Does it include the right and obligation to intervene with authority in the life of another local church? To what extent does the bishop of Rome have the obligation to listen to or to consult with other churches in making important decisions? When and how should he be criticized? We will return to some of these questions at the end of our study.

Chapter Two

NEW TESTAMENT FOUNDATIONS

Irenaeus

The patristic passage which serves best to open our discussion of the New Testament foundations for understanding the ecumenical importance of the church of Rome comes from Irenaeus.

In juxtaposing the ancient and well attested traditions of the apostles over against the new and unfounded doctrines of the heretics, Irenaeus explains the general principle that the tradition of the apostles can be found everywhere in every church in which one is able to enumerate the successors of the apostles up to the present. Then he continues:

> But since it would be very long in such a volume as this to enumerate the successions of all the churches, I can put to shame all those who in any way, whether through wicked self-conceit, or through vainglory, or through blind and evil opinion, gather as they should not [i.e. the heretics]. This I can do by pointing out (1) the tradition which that very great, oldest, and well-known church founded and established at Rome by those two most glorious [i.e. martyred] apostles Peter and Paul, received from the apostles, and (2) the faith she has announced to men, which comes down to us through the successions of bishops. For every church, i.e. the faithful from everywhere, must be in harmony with this church because of its most excellent origin; in which [church] the tradition coming from the apostles has always been preserved for the faithful from everywhere.

After the blessed apostles had founded and built up the church, they handed over the ministry of the episcopate to Linus (*Ag Her* 3.3.2–3).

In order to understand how a Greek speaking bishop from southern Gaul with strong ties to his native Asia Minor could accord to a church in Italy such an important doctrinal role in combating heresy, we need to go back in time, and place ourselves in Rome in the early decades following the martyrdom of the apostles Peter and Paul.

THE CONCORDANT MARTYRDOMS OF PETER AND PAUL

The Neronian persecution devastated the Christian community in Rome. Those who survived were deeply moved by the witness of those sisters and brothers who had been obedient unto death, and above all by the inspiring examples of the apostles Peter and Paul. After the Neronian persecution, the church in Rome was forever to be a church of the martyrs. No theology or *regula* or canon of scriptures would be accepted in this church which did not continue to support, inspire and hold high the martyrological traditions stemming from Jerusalem and above all the example of the master martyr. Thereafter, it was impossible for any bishop to give effective leadership to the Christian community in Rome without appealing to the united apostolic authority of both Peter and Paul. Nothing less than a unifying theology and a martyr's canon could have survived this mad attempt to bring to naught the Christian community in Rome. The memory of the martyrdom of the apostle Paul and the memory of the martyrdom of the apostle Peter became constitutive *of* and *for* the life of the post-Neronian church in Rome.

Each of these apostles had died for the sake of the same gospel. Their common witness to the atoning power of that gospel provided the only viable basis for any ecclesiology that would do justice to the experience of those Christians who survived this imperial persecution.

This, and this alone, explains why, until this day, the church of Rome insists on an annual joint commemoration of the martyrdom of the apostles Peter and Paul.

No Christian who spent any time in Rome following this persecution could escape the evidence of the unified apostolic witness of the two most glorious apostles Peter and Paul. Irenaeus, from Asia Minor and Gaul, is a case in point. His teacher Polycarp is another, and so on, back, we may presume, to the very early days immediately following the Neronian persecution. Irenaeus and Polycarp stood in a tradition of first-hand personal experience of the faith and hope of the church in Rome.

This was why Irenaeus could write that the tradition coming from the apostles had always been preserved for the faithful from everywhere by this church. It was a matter of experience. And it followed that this unified apostolic witness would be normative for all the faithful from everywhere, simply by virtue of its most excellent origins in the witness of these two most glorious apostles.

We see then that the martyrdom of Peter and Paul in Rome is constitutive of what came to be called the church. It must be borne in mind that this event in the history of the holy catholic church preceded the formation of the New Testament canon and indeed preceded the composition of some of the books of the New Testament.

It should not be surprising, therefore, if we find within the New Testament evidence which is consonant with this event, since this event appears to have been a constitutive event in the history of the church that formed this canon.

THE ACTS OF THE APOSTLES

We may begin with the passage in the Acts of the Apostles where near the end of his ministry Paul is said to be in danger of losing his life in Jerusalem. During the night the Lord stood by Paul and said, "Be of good cheer, Paul: for as thou hast testified of me in Jerusalem, so must thou bear witness *(martyrēsai)* also at Rome (Acts 23:11)." This places Paul's martyrdom in Rome within the context of salvation history. Such a scriptural passage would have opened the way for perceiving his apostolic martyrdom in Rome as standing in a martyrological tradition emanating from Jerusalem. "As in Jerusalem, so in Rome." Rome stands in scriptural continuity with Jerusalem. The basis for this continuity is clearly martyrological.

The martyrological tradition is also taken up in 1 Peter. In that letter, Rome is represented as Babylon. Babylon is that imperial city where King Nebuchadnezzar had once cast the faithful of Jerusalem into a burning fiery furnace (Dan 3:6).

1 PETER

It was a firm and faithful resistance to imperial persecution inspired by the Christ-like examples of the martyred apostles Peter and Paul which gave a special doctrinal importance to the church in Rome. In 1 Peter we read:

> Even gold passes through the assayer's fire, and more precious than perishable gold is faith which has stood the test. These trials come so that your faith may prove itself worthy of all praise, glory and honor when Jesus Christ is revealed. . . . Well you know that it was no perishable stuff, like gold or silver, that bought your freedom from the empty folly of your traditional ways. The price was paid in precious blood, as it were of a lamb without mark or blemish—the blood of Christ (1:7, 18–19).

That the sacrificial death of Christ is to be the chief model for the faithful is explicitly stated:

> Christ suffered on your behalf, and thereby left you an example; it is for you to follow in his steps. He committed no sin, he was convicted of no falsehood; when he was abused he did not retort with abuse, when he suffered he uttered no threats, but committed his cause to the One who judges justly. In his own person he carried our sins to the gibbet, so that we might cease to live for sin and begin to live for righteousness. By his wounds you have been healed. You were straying like sheep, but now you have turned toward the shepherd and guardian of your souls (2:21–25).

The linking of Christ's suffering with the suffering of the faithful is reiterated:

Keep your conscience clear, so that when you are abused, those who malign your Christian conduct may be put to shame. It is better to suffer for well-doing, if such should be the will of God, than for doing wrong. For Christ also died for our sins once and for all. He, the just, suffered for the unjust, to bring us to God. In the body he was put to death; in the spirit he was brought to life (3:16–19).

That we have here an explicit doctrine of martyrdom in which the faithful are exhorted to call to memory the bodily suffering of Christ is left in no doubt.

Remembering that Christ endured bodily suffering, you must arm yourselves with a temper of mind like his. When a man has thus endured bodily sufferings he has finished with sin, and for the rest of his days on earth he may live, not for the things that men desire, but for what God wills (4:1–2).

Persecution provides the Christian martyr an opportunity to share in Christ's suffering. And this is a cause for joy.

My dear friends, do not be bewildered by the fiery ordeal that is upon you, as though it were something extraordinary. It gives you a share in Christ's sufferings, and that is cause for joy; and when his glory is revealed, your joy will be triumphant. If Christ's name is flung in your teeth as an insult, count yourselves blessed, because then that glorious Spirit which is the Spirit of God is resting upon you (4:12–15).

Although this letter is written out of personal experience of the redemptive power of innocent suffering, it bears an electric message of warning and hope for all Christians who are facing persecution.

Awake! Be on the alert! Your enemy the devil, like a roaring lion, prowls around looking for someone to devour. Stand up to him, firm in faith, and remember that your brother Christians are going through the same kinds of suffering while they are in the world. And the God of all grace, who called you into his eternal glory in Christ, will himself, after your brief sufferings, restore, establish, and strengthen you on a firm foundation. He holds dominion for ever and ever. Amen (5:8–11).

POLYCARP AND IGNATIUS

Polycarp in Asia would have gladly read this earlier letter from the church in Rome as offering inspiring evidence of the apostolic witness of the holy catholic faith. Members of the Christian family scattered in the world, dwelling temporarily in various places, were bound together by this common faith. Providentially there was a center from which a word of hope continued to emanate. That center was the church "which dwells in Babylon" (5:13). Polycarp was not left to simply hearing this apostolic letter from Rome read and reread in the church at Smyrna, nor to reading it for himself. He could do more. He could go to Rome. He could taste first-hand and test the faith of that church. And this he did. Not with hat in hand. For Polycarp represented the church in Asia. He brought with him to Rome the faith of the apostles as it was celebrated in Asia.

In coming to Rome Polycarp stood in an apostolic tradition which had already learned to celebrate the concordant witness that Peter and Paul had made. In his letter to the church in Rome, Ignatius, at an earlier time while staying over with Polycarp in Smyrna, had written:

I do not enjoin you, as Peter and Paul did. They were apostles, I am a convict; they were free, but I am a slave to this very hour. Yet if I shall suffer, then I am a freedman of Jesus Christ, and I shall rise free in him (4).

This reference to being a freedman of Jesus Christ is taken from the witness of Paul (1 Cor 7:22) and united with the witness of Peter (1 Pet 1:18–19). Paul reminds the Corinthians that they were "bought at a price" (1 Cor 7:23). Peter specifies that the price of freedom is the blood of Christ (1 Pet 1:19). By suffering one attains this freedom in Christ.

> Now I am learning in my bonds to put away every desire. From Syria even unto Rome I fight with wild beasts. . . . Come fire and cross and grapplings with wild beasts, wrenching of bones, hacking of limbs, crushings of my whole body, come cruel torture of the devil to assail me. Only be it mine to attain to Jesus Christ (Ign, *Rom,* 4–5).

In summary, Ignatius knows of the concordant apostolic witness of Peter and Paul to the church in Rome. He knows that though he is not an apostle, yet will he be free if he suffers with Christ. Though the devil (like a roaring lion) assail him, yet will he attain unto Jesus Christ.

Ignatius proceeds to his climax:

> Him I seek, who died on our behalf; him I desire, who rose again [for our sake]. The pangs of a new birth are upon me. . . . Permit me to be an imitator of the passion of my God (6).

Ignatius, moving to his conclusion, beseeches the church in Rome to pray for the church in Syria, and observes:

> Jesus Christ alone shall be its bishop—he and your love (9, i.e. the love of the church in Rome [including its willingness to permit Ignatius to be an imitator of the passion of Christ], united with Jesus Christ himself, will lead the church in Syria in the absence of its bishop).

Imitating the words of Paul, Ignatius continues:

> But for myself I am ashamed to be called one of them (a bishop); for I do not deserve it, being the very least of

them and an untimely birth (1 Cor 15:8, 9); yet by his mercy I shall be someone, if, that is, I attain unto God (9).

Polycarp, the teacher of Irenaeus and close episcopal colleague of Ignatius, received 1 Peter in good faith and was effective in uniting apostolic tradition from the Johannine circle in Asia with the apostolic martyrological tradition from Rome. This is clear from his letter to the church which "sojourned in Philippi."

> For everyone *who shall not confess that Jesus Christ is come in the flesh, is antichrist* (1 Jn 4:2–4): and whosoever shall not confess the testimony of the Cross is *of the devil* (1 Jn 3:8; cf. Jn 8:44); and whosoever shall pervert the oracles of the Lord to his own lusts and say that there is neither resurrection nor judgment, that man is the firstborn of Satan (7). . . . Let us therefore without ceasing hold fast by our hope and by the earnest of our righteousness, which is Jesus Christ who *took up our sins in his own body upon the tree* (cf. 1 Pet 2:24) *who did no sin, neither was guile found in his mouth* (1 Pet 2:22), but for our sakes he endured all things, *that we might live in him* (cf. 1 Jn 4:9). Let us therefore become imitators of his endurance; *and if we should suffer for his name's sake, let us glorify him* (cf. 1 Pet 4:16). For he gave his example to us in his own person, and we believed this (8).

Polycarp saw the endurance of Ignatius, whose eyes were steadfast on Rome, as an example of obedience to the martyrological example of Jesus, and he was able to unite all this with the experience of the Philippian church with martyrdom, and with the martyrological example of Paul and the rest of the apostles.

> I exhort you all therefore to be obedient unto the word of righteousness and to practice all endurance, which also ye saw with your own eyes in the blessed Ignatius and Zosimus and Rufus, yes in others who came from

among yourselves, as well as in Paul himself and the rest of the apostles; being persuaded that all these *ran not in vain* (Phil 2:16; cf. Gal 2:2) but in faith and righteousness, and that they are *in their due place* (cf. *1 Clem* 5), in the presence of the Lord, *with whom also they suffered* (cf. Rom 8:17). For they *loved not the present world* (contrast Demas, 2 Tim 4:10), but *him that died for our sakes and was raised by God for us* (cf. Ign, *Rom* 6; 2 Cor 5:15; 1 Thes 5:10). Stand fast therefore in these things and follow the example of the Lord, *being firm in the faith* (cf. Ign, *Eph* 10; Col 1:23; 1 Cor 15:58; 1 Pet 5:9 [9–10]).

The rare expression translated "in their due place" is copied by Polycarp (or derived by him) from *1 Clement* 5, where it is used in reference to the apostle Peter[1] in a classic passage in which Peter and Paul are cited by Clement as noble examples of apostles who were persecuted and "contended even unto death."

1 CLEMENT

"The Martyrdom of Peter and Paul"

But not to dwell on ancient examples, let us come to the most recent spiritual heroes. Let us take the noble examples furnished in our own generation. Through envy and jealousy, the greatest and most righteous pillars [of the church] have been persecuted and put to death. Let us set before our eyes the good apostles [Peter and Paul]. Peter, through unrighteous envy, endured not one or two, but numerous labours; and when he had at length suffered martyrdom, departed to the place of glory due to him. Owing to envy, Paul also obtained the reward of patient endurance, after being seven times thrown into captivity, compelled to flee, and stoned. After perishing in both the east and the west, he won the noble renown which his faith merited. He taught righteousness to the whole world, and having come to the highest point of the west, he suffered martyrdom before the rulers. And so, released from this world, he was taken up into the holy place and became the greatest example of patient endurance (5).

Out of deference to the church in Corinth which also regarded itself as having been founded by Peter and Paul, Clement of Rome makes no explicit reference to the place where these two apostles both rendered their "obedience unto death." But the whole procedure, where the church in Rome is exercising a responsibility to intervene in the internal affairs of the church in Corinth, presupposes that some enormous transformation in the relationship between the churches in these two Roman cities has taken place. That one is in Rome and the other is in a colony of Rome simply cannot be the explanation for this astounding development in church polity. Jesus had said to his disciples: "You know that in the world, rulers lord it over their subjects, and their great men make them feel the weight of authority; but it shall not be so with you" (Mt 20:25–26).

The most satisfactory explanation for the facts as we know them is that the church in Rome is exercising an authority which proceeds from its vocation to live out of the united witness of these two "good" apostles (as Clement so gently puts it), and to help other churches do the same. And how will this authority be exercised? As Clement indicates in his letter from the church in Rome it will be by *agape*. "What shall we do, then, brethren? Shall we become slothful in welldoing, and cease from the practice of love? God forbid! . . . let us work the work of righteousness with our whole strength" (33).

Jesus had gone on to say to his disciples:

Among you
   Whoever wants to be great
      Must be your servant.
And
   Whoever wants to be first
      Must be servant of all

For
>The Son of Man did not come to be served
>>But to serve
>And to give up his life
>>As a ransom for the many (Mt 20:26b–28/Mk
>>10:43b–45).

Clement carries his readers to the heart of the matter in the sixteenth chapter of his letter:

Christ is of those who are truly humble and not of those who exalt themselves over his flock. Our Lord Jesus Christ, the sceptre of God's majesty, did not come in the pomp of pride or arrogance, although he might have done so. But he came in a lowly condition, as the Holy Spirit had declared regarding him. For he says:

"Lord, who hath believed our report, and to whom is the
>arm of the Lord revealed?
We have declared [our message] in his presence:
He is, as it were, a child, and like a root in thirsty ground;
He has no form nor glory. . . .
He is a man exposed to stripes and suffering, and
>acquainted with the endurance of grief;
For his countenance was turned away;
He was despised and not esteemed.
He bears our iniquities, and is in sorrow for our sakes.
. . . .
But he was wounded for our transgressions, and bruised for
>our iniquities.
To bring us peace he was punished; by his stripes we were
>healed.
All we, like sheep, have gone astray; every one has
>wandered in his own way;
And the Lord has delivered him up for our sins.
While in the midst of his sufferings, he openeth not his
>mouth.
He was brought a sheep to the slaughter, and as a lamb
>before his shearer is dumb,

So he openeth not his mouth.
In his humiliation his condemnation ended; who shall
   declare his generation?
For his life was taken away from the earth.
For the transgressions of my people he was brought down
   to death.
And I will give the wicked as an offering for his burial and
   the rich for his death.
For he did no iniquity, neither was guile found in his
   mouth. . . .
On this account he shall have many heirs, and shall share
   the spoils of the strong;
Because his soul was delivered to death, and he was found
   among the transgressors,
And he bore the sins of many, and for their sins he was
   delivered up" (Is 53).

And again he says:

"I am a worm, and no man; a reproach of men, and
   despised of the people.
All that see me have derided me; they have spoken with
   their lips;
they have wagged their heads [saying] he hoped in God, let
   God deliver him,
but God saved him, since he delighted in him" (Ps 22).

You see, beloved, what is the example which has been
given us; for if the Lord thus humbled himself, what
shall we do who have through him come under the yoke
of His grace? (16).

Well past the middle of his letter to the church in Corinth,
the bishop of the church in Rome, in obedience to the vocation
of his church, turns the attention of the church in Corinth to the
words of the apostle Paul: "Take up the epistle of the blessed Paul
the Apostle. What wrote he first unto you in the beginning of the
Gospel?" (47). What follows in Clement's letter is an unmistak-
able reference to 1 Corinthians 1:10–12.

1 Corinthians

> Now I beseech you, brethren, by the name of our Lord Jesus Christ, that all of you come to agreement and that there be no divisions among you; and that you be perfectly joined together in the same mind and in the same judgment. For it has been brought to my attention concerning you, my sisters and brothers, by the people of Chloe, that there are some contentions among you. It boils down to this: some of you are saying "I am of Paul," others "I am of Apollos," others "I am of Cephas," and still others "I am of Christ." Is Christ divided? Was Paul crucified for you? Or were you baptized in the name of Paul (1:10–13).

Clement makes use of this passage to address a current problem in the Corinthian church concerning disunity over the authority of elders. But if we are to understand the apostolic power of Paul, and the authority of the bishop of Rome in calling on the authority of Paul in this instance, not only must we bear in mind that Clement writes from the church in which Paul's martyrdom (concordant with that of Peter) is constitutive of its very being, but also we must bear in mind the central message of this formative letter as a whole. The central message of 1 Corinthians is that of the gospel of the crucified and risen Christ silently undergirded by the normative authority of Isaiah 53.

> For Christ sent me not to baptize, but to preach the gospel: not with wisdom of words, lest the cross of Christ should be made of no effect. For the preaching of the cross is to them that perish foolishness; but unto us who are being saved it is the power of God (1:17–18).

After developing this theme at great length, Paul turns to the topic of his own experiences in order to bring his readers under the authority of a suffering Christ:

> I think that God hath set forth us apostles last, as it were appointed to death: for we are made a spectacle unto the

world, and to angels, and to men. We are fools for
Christ's sake, but ye are wise in Christ; we are weak, but
ye are strong; ye are honorable, but we are despised.
Even unto this present hour we both hunger, and thirst,
and are naked, and are buffeted, and have no certain
dwelling place; and labor, working with our hands:
being reviled, we bless; being persecuted, we suffer it;
being defamed, we entreat: we are made as the filth of
the world, and are the offscouring of all things unto this
day. I write these things not to shame you, but as my
beloved children I warn you. For though you have ten
thousand instructors in Christ, yet you have not many
fathers; for in Christ Jesus I have begotten you through
the gospel. Wherefore I beseech you, be ye imitators of
me (4:9–16).

Next comes the passage in which Paul's apostolic presence
in Corinth through his letter is backed up by an announcement
of the imminent arrival of Paul's emissary. This passage helps us
to understand, if not anticipate, the development which has led
to Clement's intervention in the name of the apostle into the
internal affairs of the church in Corinth. What is new is the meaning now borne by Paul's exhortation: "Be ye imitators of me."
These words now bear the full weight (for those who would
accept it) of his faithful obedience unto death. This letter from
the church of Rome will have as much authority in Corinth as
the Corinthian Christians accord to a church which is now living
out of the martyrological tradition represented by the concordant
deaths of Paul and Peter in Rome.

For this cause have I sent unto you Timothy, who is my
beloved son, and faithful in the Lord, who shall bring
you into remembrance of my ways which be in Christ,
as I teach everywhere in every church (4:17).

Paul next deals at length with a difficult set of practical problems in the Corinthian church which leads him ultimately to the

topic of the eucharist:

> The cup of blessing which we bless, is it not the com-
> munion of the blood of Christ? The bread which we
> break, is it not the communion of the body of Christ?
> For we being many are one bread, and one body: for we
> are all partakers of that one bread (10:16–17).

After expostulating from this premise on the problems facing
the Corinthian church Paul once again appeals to his own example and concludes: "Be ye imitators of me, as I am of Christ"
(11:1).

Paul then takes up another set of problems which leads him
to the topic of the Lord's supper.

With reference to the Lord's supper Paul wrote as follows:

> The tradition which I handed on to you [concerning the
> Lord's supper], originated with the Lord himself. That
> tradition is [I need not remind you] that: "The Lord
> Jesus, during the night in which he was delivered up,
> took bread. And after giving thanks, he broke it and
> said: 'This is my body, which is for you; do this in
> remembrance of me.' In the same way, after supper he
> took the cup, saying 'This cup is the new covenant in
> my blood. Do this, as often as you drink it, in remem-
> brance of me. For as often as you eat this bread and
> drink the cup, you proclaim the death of the Lord, until
> he comes'" (11:23–26).

In order to understand the relationship between Peter and
Paul, and the importance of that relationship for our understanding the origin and significance of 1 Corinthians 11:23–26, we can
begin by asking: "By what authority does the apostle to the Gentiles assure the Corinthian church that the tradition concerning
the Lord's supper he had received and had in turn passed on to
them, originated with Jesus himself?" Paul would never have

claimed that he was an eyewitness to what happened during the night in which Jesus was delivered up. Nor can we understand him to be claiming that this is a tradition that had been revealed to him bodily and verbally by revelation from the risen Christ. All the technical terminology used by Paul indicates that this tradition, like that concerning the resurrection appearances he mentions later (15:3–7), has been handed on as a well-formulated statement in the conventional manner of the time.[2]

It is most likely that, in the first instance, Paul received these vital traditions he passed on to his churches from the church he had persecuted before he became a Christian. But in matters as important as these, it is not unlikely that Paul took pains to be sure about what he was authorizing his churches to receive as tradition concerning the normative events of the gospel.

In the case of the tradition concerning the resurrection appearances, Paul had his own direct experience of the risen Christ to serve as a control by which to judge the tradition he had received. And it is clear that he knows, or at least firmly believes, that the appearance of the risen Lord to him is of the same order as that to the other apostles.

Paul tells the Corinthians that most of the over five hundred brethren to whom the Lord appeared on a single occasion were still alive at the time of writing (15:6). While it is possible, indeed probable, that Paul had the opportunity both preceding and following his conversion, to discuss the resurrection of Jesus with some of these Christians, this would hardly have satisfied the unquestioned concern for truth regarding events of the past that were decisive for the pastoral and theological task of expediting the gospel, which we know motivated Paul (cf. Gal 1:20; 2:5, 14).

Since the tradition he had received concerning the resurrection placed Peter and the twelve at the beginning of the series of resurrection appearances, to have discussed these appearances with Peter would have been of importance to Paul. Did Paul have the opportunity to hear anything directly from Peter on these matters, or on matters bearing on Paul's belief that the resurrection appearances to Peter and the other apostles were of the same order as his? The answer is: "He certainly did."

GALATIANS

In his letter to the churches of Galatia, Paul informs his readers that three years after his conversion he went up (from Damascus) to Jerusalem to visit (or get to know) Peter. And he adds that he remained with Peter fifteen days (1:18).

In order to begin to comprehend the far-reaching consequences of this meeting it is necessary to answer certain questions. Granting that Paul presumably wanted to make contact with church authorities in Jerusalem (he did see James, for example), why did he go to Peter? And why did he remain with Peter fifteen days?

We need to address the second question first. In doing so, we shall ask what we can learn from a philological analysis of the text about the probable parameters of Paul's purpose or purposes in undertaking this history making trip. We face three main tasks. The first is to ascertain as best we can what Paul had been doing during the three year period between his return to Damascus mentioned in verse 17 and his visit to Peter referred to in verse 18. The second is to determine the most probable meaning in this context of the verb Paul used that is generally rendered in English by "to visit" or "to get to know." The third is to analyze the verbal phrase "and I remained with him" in relation to the temporal phrase "for fifteen days."

The Previous Three Years' Activity

The first task presents no great difficulties. Paul tells us in verse 21 that after he had finished his business in Jerusalem he set out for the regions of Syria and Cilicia and that at that time he was still unknown by face to the churches of Christ in Judea (22). What these churches knew about him was only what they could learn from the reports they heard about him, and these reports were to the effect that "the one who formerly persecuted us now preaches the faith he formerly ravished" (23). To which Paul simply adds: "And they (i.e. those whom Paul formerly persecuted) glorified God in me" (24). Where were these Christians who glorified God in Paul?

Beginning in v. 16 Paul tells his readers that (contrary to

what they may have heard from others) following his conversion he did not immediately confer with flesh and blood, nor did he go up to Jerusalem to [make contact with] those who were apostles before him, but rather he went away into Arabia, and then (without specifying how long he remained in Arabia) he adds: "and I returned again to Damascus" (17). This clearly implies that Paul had been in or near Damascus at the time of his conversion. Since the churches of Christ in Judea did not know Paul by face, but only by reports they heard from others, it is clear that Paul had been preaching the gospel in some area outside Judea during the three year interval in question, and it presents the least difficulty if we conclude that he had been doing this in and around Damascus, or perhaps more broadly in the general area of southern Syria. It had to be in some place outside Judea, some place where his earlier persecuting activity was still vividly remembered and could be existentially juxtaposed to his present activity.

Since in verse 21 Paul writes that upon leaving Jerusalem he went into the regions of Syria and Cilicia, and then includes not one word about what he did for the next fourteen years before returning to Jerusalem for the apostolic conference of Galatians 2:1-10, we are to conclude that the terse phrase "into the regions of Syria and Cilicia" is directional and that Paul is opening up a new phase of his missionary career that at least in its initial stage was to see him through the Cilician gates. Paul would in any case most probably have come into Galatia from Cilicia. Once the Galatians came to know Paul they would have had reason to follow his career with interest. But where Paul had been before he came to Galatia from Syria and Cilicia would have been relatively vague to them. The one thing they did not know and needed to get straight was Paul's earliest contacts with the Jerusalem based apostles. This explains Paul's relatively detailed account on this point. From this account we can infer a great deal more than he explicitly tells us.

From our analysis we conclude that during the three years in question, Paul had been preaching the gospel outside Judea in an area of his former persecuting activity, and that during this period of evangelization he had laid the groundwork for beginning a westward mission to the Gentiles. His going to Jerusalem of a necessity must have proceeded from the reality of these three years of preaching and from his decision to embark on this far-reaching mission.

To Visit Cephas

In verse 18 Paul explains that he went up to Jerusalem to visit Peter. The verb used is *historēsai* which in this case can be best understood if we begin with its cognate noun form *histōr*. The *histōr* in ancient Greece functioned as examiner and arbiter in legal matters. He was learned in the law and skilled in examining witnesses. He knew how to ask the right questions of people who were being examined in order to ascertain the truth in matters of dispute. The truth he was after was not philosophical truth in some abstract metaphysical sense, but rather the kind of truth that can issue in practical wisdom. In the final analysis the *histōr* would be called upon to make a judgment. The *histōr* was a judge.

The first Greek historians were geographers who explored the great rivers that emptied into the known seas. Having penetrated inland as far as they could safely travel, they would then interrogate people who had come down these rivers from further inland to get from them eyewitness accounts about the unexplored sources of the great rivers running further back up into the unknown interiors of the continents. These same Greeks would question the priests living in the temples, which were supported by these ancient river cultures, about records kept in the temples, about the genealogies of the local kings, and about the customs of the local inhabitants. The reports of these geographers constituted the beginnings of what came to be called "history."

The verb *historēsai* can mean to inquire into or about a thing, or to inquire about a person. Or it can also mean to "examine" or to "observe." Such a questioner or observer would then become "one who is informed" about something, or "one who knows."

In the case at hand the verb is used with the accusative of person, so that it can mean to "inquire of" or "to ask." One can inquire of an oracle. Lexicographers are led to place our text in this context and cite Galatians 1:18 as follows: "*visit* a person *(Cephas)* for the purpose of inquiry." Such a meaning is contextually preferable to those one generally finds in English translations: R.S.V. "visit"; N.E.B. "get to know"; Goodspeed "become acquainted with"; or the amplified New Testament "become (personally) acquainted with." Even the paraphrase "visit Cephas *for the purpose of inquiry*" is lexicographically limited in that it fails to suggest as strongly as it might the well-established usages: "examine" and "observe," both of which are faithful to the function of the *histōr* and open up rich possibilities for understanding what Paul meant and how his readers would have understood his phrasing in this instance.

The linguistic evidence examined thus far by no means limits us to a view that Paul meant to suggest that he had simply made a courtesy call or that he went up to Jerusalem for an innocuous social visit with Peter. As we go deeper into the lexicographical evidence offered by Liddell and Scott, we are carried even farther away from such an understanding of the text.[3] The word, of course, can mean simply "to visit." But should we so understand it in the context in which we find it?

The most complete study of *historēsai* as used by Paul has been made by G.D. Kilpatrick.[4] Kilpatrick takes into consideration the Latin, Coptic and Syriac versions, all of which understand *historēsai* in the sense of "to see." He notes, however, that later commentators were not content with this interpretation. Chrysostom perceived that *historēsai* must here mean more than "see." He makes a distinction between *eidein* (to see) and *historēsai* and explicitly notes that Paul does not write: *eidein Petron,* but *historēsai Petron.* Kilpatrick discusses the views of other writers, Greek and Latin, and concludes that the oldest identifiable interpretation is that of the versions which treat *historēsai* as the equivalent of *eidein* and dates it to the second century. Chrysostom's comment, which is shared by Latin commentators, he dates as earlier than the middle of the fourth century, and suggests that it perhaps belongs to the Antiochene tradition of exegesis.

On the basis of Liddell and Scott's article which Kilpatrick regards as probably the best guide we have, but also taking into account other lexicographical aids, he concludes that "*historēsai Kēphan* at Galatians 1:18 is to be taken as meaning 'to get information from Cephas.'"[5] In coming to this conclusion Kilpatrick notes that the reason that ancient commentators rejected this interpretation is that it appeared to them to be "inapplicable" in Paul's case. On the basis of Galatians 1:11-12, where Paul says that he received "the gospel" by revelation, "they argued that St. Paul had already received the requisite knowledge by revelation and so had no need to visit St. Peter for that purpose." Those who took this position, and at the same time recognized that *historēsai* must mean more than *eidein,* generally followed Chrysostom in making Paul visit Peter "to pay his respects." Kilpatrick notes that for Augustine the visit was merely a token of friendship. For Victorinus and Ambrosiaster the visit is an acknowledgement of "the primacy of Peter."[6]

Kilpatrick has his own theory as to why Paul would have sought information from Peter. He notes that the interpretation suggested by Liddell and Scott "to visit a person for purpose of inquiry," i.e. "to get information," satisfied the conditions of the context, so long as the meaning of *evangellion* does not mean "information about Jesus," and since Paul seeks information from Peter and not from James, with whom he also had some contact, Kilpatrick asks: "Is there any information that one had to give him that the other could not provide?" In answer he writes: "St. Peter had been an eyewitness and disciple of Jesus. St. James could not claim to be a comparable informant about the teaching and the ministry." In conclusion Kilpatrick writes: "We know then of one kind of information for which St. Paul would go to St. Peter rather than St. James, information about Jesus' teaching and ministry."

Kilpatrick considers but rejects the first meaning that Liddell and Scott give, "that of inquiry into or about a person or thing (p. 147)." He cites Plutarch for an example of the use of *historēsai* for "getting information" about both persons and things.[7] "Aristippus is so excited by what he hears of Socrates that he is beside himself. . . . He found out about the man, his utterances and his philosophy." For some unaccountable reason, Kilpatrick dismisses the lexicographical implications of this text from a near contemporary of Paul by saying, "But we may exclude at once the explanation that *historēsai Kēphan* meant 'to inquire into, investigate, Cephas'." In fact "to get information from Cephas" is not incompatible with "to inquire into, investigate Cephas." Because of the very close relationship of Peter to Jesus, and because Jesus first appeared to Peter, for Paul to go to Peter for information about Jesus' teaching and ministry entails from the outset that Paul is involved in questioning Peter not only about Jesus, but in effect about Peter's memory of Jesus, his beliefs about the meaning of Jesus' death and resurrection, and thus Peter as a witness is inextricably bound up together with that to which he is a witness. The two cannot be separated as simply as Kilpatrick suggests. We see no objection to combining Liddell and Scott's first meaning for *historēsai* with their suggested interpretation. To be sure the focus of Paul's inquiry would be Jesus, but that can hardly have precluded serious attention by Paul to the question of Peter's credibility. Indeed we may say that the apostolic witness preserved in the New Testament rests primarily upon Paul's conviction of Peter's credibility as a witness, as well as upon Peter's conviction of Paul's credibility as a witness. Their mutuality in finding one another to be credible witnesses is absolutely basic for understanding Christian origins.

At issue is how we are to understand certain phrases Paul uses in arguing for his independence of the authority of the Jerusalem apostles, or as he refers to them "those who were apostles before me" (Gal 1:17). The translators of the New English Bible have a firm grasp of the essential character of Paul's argument, so we can best follow his thought by citing that translation. In his opening words Paul strikes this note of apostolic independence: "From Paul, an apostle, not by human appointment or human commission, but by commission from Jesus Christ and from God the Father who raised him from the dead" (Gal 1:1). To remind his readers that Jesus Christ has been raised from the dead by God the Father immediately places Paul who has seen the risen Jesus on an equal footing with all the other apostles and cuts the ground out from any argument that would proceed from some presumed advantage on the part of those apostles who had known Jesus before his death and resurrection.

"I must make it clear to you, my friends, that the gospel you heard me preach is no human invention. I did not take it from any man [not from Peter or James for example]; no man taught it me; I received it through a revelation of Jesus Christ" (Gal 1:11–12).

Paul is not denying that he has ever taken over anything from anyone, least of all is he denying that he has ever been taught by anyone. The fact that in his first letter to the Corinthians he explicitly states that he is handing on a tradition that he had received—"that Christ died for our sins, in accordance with the scriptures"—makes it clear that there was tradition, including factual information concerning Jesus that Paul did receive. But for Paul facts themselves do not the gospel make. No doubt Paul, as a Pharisee of the Pharisees, in his role as persecutor of the church, made himself acquainted with the essential content of the gospel as it was being preached and defended by those within the covenant community with whom he was contending. Indeed it would not be out of character for this great theologian to have achieved an even more firm and comprehensive grasp of the essential content of this gospel than was in the head of many of the faithful who were willing to die for it. What was at issue for Paul was not the factual content of the gospel, but its truth, including of course the truth of its factual content. As he persecuted the church and ravished the faith, he was convinced that the gospel preached by the Christians was false. That is why he was willing to persecute them unto death if necessary. Everything hinges on the "truth of the gospel." Once it pleased God to reveal his Son to Paul, so that Paul could see Jesus as the Son of God, everything changed (see Gal 1:12, 15; 1 Cor 9:1; 15:8; Phil 3:21). What had been perceived as false was now recognized as true on the basis of Christ's appearance to Paul. That in essence is the nature of Paul's conversion. The factual basis of Christian faith did not change. For example, that Jesus had died, or even that he had been crucified, was never in dispute between the Christians and the pre-Christian Paul. But the belief that Jesus had died "for the sins" of others, "according to the scriptures"—that was a faith claim made by the church whose truth the pre-Christian Paul could never have accepted, but whose truth, on the basis of Christ's resurrection appearance to him, he was now prepared to embrace, pass on to his converts, and presumably himself proclaim. That there were factual details concerning these deep matters of faith that may have interested Paul should not cause alarm for those who wish, at all costs, to preserve his independence of those eyewitnesses upon whom he would have been dependent for finding adequate answers to some of his questions.

We take this position because the answers Paul received were always received within the context of a faith already firmly and irrevocably grounded in the decisive revelation that preceded and led to his questions. Most if not all of Paul's post-conversion questions would have been of the nature of questions for the purpose of clarification in detail. Paul would hardly have asked Peter "Did Jesus die?" or "Was Jesus crucified?" That kind of information would have been contained in the essential kerygma Paul had formerly rejected and now himself proclaimed.

Paul's pre-Christian questioning would have focused on issues vital to the way in which the law and the prophets were being interpreted and acted upon. But once Paul became a Christian there would have been a whole new set of questions for him to ask concerning aspects of Christian life and faith which were relatively untouched by points at issue over whether something had or had not happened "in accordance with the scriptures." As a Pharisee Paul had sat in Moses' seat, and it thus had been for him and his fellow Pharisees to decide how the law and prophets were to be interpreted. When any members of the covenant were interpreting the law and the prophets in a manner contrary to Pharisaic teaching, and especially when these interpretations led to behavior that was threatening to the established world of Jewish piety, Paul, as a Pharisee, zealous for the law, was constrained to act. And act he did. But once Paul was converted, questions like "What happened on the night Jesus was handed over?"—i.e. questions concerning matters important to Christians, but which had not been problem-causing to Paul the enforcer of torah— would now have become questions of interest to Paul the Christian leader and they were perfectly legitimate questions for him to pursue. As his leadership role in the church grew, that he have a firm grasp on such matters would have assumed some place of importance, however minor, in Paul's overall preparation for mission.

In this context we should not shy away from accepting the

plain meaning of what Paul writes in reference to going to Jerusalem: he went to question Peter. Paul is not making himself subservient to anyone in his decision to ask questions. This apostolic concern to "get it right" is foundational for Christian life and faith. Paul is not forensically diminishing his authority by "making inquiry" of Peter. On the contrary his use of *historēsai* in this context conceptually places Peter in the dock. Paul is the *histōr*. Peter is the one being cross-examined. What is at issue is the truth in a whole range of practical matters which Paul wants to discuss with Peter—none, we conclude, extending to the heart of his gospel. That much Paul appears to rule out decisively in what he says about how he received his gospel in Galatians 1:1–17.

Paul, in going to Jerusalem to question Peter, is moving up the stream of church tradition to its very source, i.e. to those eyewitnesses who first carefully formulated it.

Paul's use of *historēsai* at this point serves very well his purpose of establishing both his apostolic independence and his apostolic authority. He is not just an independent apostle who has seen the risen Jesus. *He is an independent apostle who stands in a close relationship to Peter.* By implication, everything that Paul did or said in the church after that meeting carried with it the implicit authority of both Paul and Peter. That was the risk Peter took in agreeing to the meeting. We have no way of knowing from any statement made by Peter on the subject how Peter viewed Paul's coming to Jerusalem. But the practice of risk-taking out of love, even love of a potential enemy, has been endemic to Christian faith from its origin in the heart of Jesus.

"And I Remained with Him Fifteen Days"

The conventional critical comment on this clause reflects the purpose of this clause in Paul's overall argument in Galatians, namely, to establish that he was not dependent for his authority to preach the gospel upon those who had been apostles before him. Thus Ernest De Witt Burton writes: "The mention of the brief duration of the stay is intended, especially in contrast with the three years of absence from Jerusalem, to show how impossible it was to regard him as a disciple of the Twelve, learning all that he knew of the Gospel from them."[8] But if this is the case, how much more remarkable is the evidence that Paul provides! For in this case Paul's statement that he remained with Peter for fifteen days is being given under some constraint. His purpose would have been better served had he been able to write that the visit was for only one day.

We have an example in the early church of such a one day visit which features "greeting the brethren" (Acts 21:7). Of course such visits can last several days. Thus when King Agrippa and Bernice arrived at Caesarea for a courtesy visit to Festus, "They spent several days there" (Acts 25:13–14). While visits in the early church are often for unspecified periods of time, it is not unusual to have the length of stay explicitly mentioned, and it is instructive to see Paul's visit with Peter against the background of a spectrum of visits of specified length. Thus in addition to the one day visit of Acts 21:7, there are three instances of seven day stays or stayovers. Thus Paul met up at Troas with some fellow workers who had gone on ahead, and they spent a week there. This is not a visit per se, but it is instructive (Acts 20:6). As Paul was returning to Jerusalem for the last time his ship put in at Tyre to unload cargo. He took advantage of the situation and spent seven days with the disciples in that city before returning to his ship (Acts 21:4). On his way to Rome Paul and those with him finally reached the port of Puteoli, where some fellow Christians invited them to remain with them seven days (Acts 28:14).

If we are to appreciate the significance of Paul's two week stay with Peter, we cannot do better than recognize that in cultures which observe a lunar calendar important meetings or conferences fall into one or another of four basic categories.

There are important one day visits. These provide the occasion for direct face to face meetings between important persons. Only limited tasks can be accomplished, however, during a one day meeting.

Next we have a basic pattern of three days and two nights. The guests arrive during the first day, and after greetings and preliminary matters are taken care of, the agenda for the following day is agreed upon. What is not accomplished during the second day can be dealt with before departure on the third day. The three day visit, meeting, or conference is very efficient and often used.

Next is the one week meeting. This is reserved for more

important meetings. For one thing it is very expensive in terms of time taken out of the busy schedules of the persons concerned, as well as the time required in making arrangements for such a long series of discussions. A great deal can be accomplished within the rhythm of the week long meeting.

It is relatively rare, however, for conferences, whether planned or unplanned, to go into a second week. Such two week conferences, when planned, are generally arranged some time in advance, and are reserved for only the most long-term projects. A fifteen day visit corresponds comfortably to the rhythm of a two week conference. One could arrive on the sixth day of the week sometime before sunset which begins the sabbath and depart early on the morning following the sabbath two weeks later. Such a stay will accommodate a leisurely visit, with ample time for work and relaxation. One can expect maximum communication during such a visit. Among other things such a period of time allows for the most difficult of topics to be laid out on the table, and, providing the persons concerned are capable of it, there is time to confront decisive issues, bear mounting tensions, and confidently await lasting resolutions, all within the framework of what can be called a "double sabbath."

The point is not that Peter and Paul used their two week visit in any such fashion. We will never know how they spent those days together in Jerusalem. The point is that two weeks for important leaders, not to say the two persons who eventually emerged as the two leading apostles of the church, is a considerable length of time for a visit. Seldom do great leaders have the luxury of such schedules. In our own time one thinks of the Camp David accords. Or we can cite the two week visit that Dietrich Bonhoeffer made to talk with Karl Barth on his way back from his stay in the United States before he took up his role within the life of the Third Reich, which led eventually to his death.

Two weeks provided ample time for both Peter and Paul to discuss whatever was uppermost in their minds, including such topics, we must presume, as the Lord's supper and other matters bearing upon the preaching of the gospel, including the resurrection.

And when we realize the full range of meanings that Paul's readers could rightfully associate with his use of *historēsai* in this context, presuming that he was careful in his choice of language, we must be open to understanding Paul as saying that he went to Jerusalem to question, examine and observe, to the end that he would leave informed and ready to report to others on the results of his inquiry.

Peter was Paul's host throughout the two week period. As Peter's guest Paul was being afforded an unparalleled opportunity to gain an inside view of Peter's life and manners. To remain with Peter for two weeks would, of necessity, have afforded them the opportunity to share table fellowship, and it is altogether likely that they observed the Lord's supper together in accordance with the words of institution which are preserved for us in 1 Corinthians 11:23–26 sometime during that two week period. It would be interesting to know whether James was present on this presumed occasion.

We are now ready to take up the question with which we began this section on Galatians. Granting that Paul wanted to make contact with church authorities in Jerusalem (he did see James, for example), why did he go to Peter?

The Role of Peter in the Pre-Pauline Palestinian Church

In the gospel of Matthew are preserved in their pristine oral form the following words of Jesus:

> Woe unto you, Chorazin!
>   Woe unto you, Bethsaida!
>   For if the mighty works which were done in you
>   Had been in Tyre and Sidon
>   They would have repented long ago in sackcloth
>   and ashes.
>   But I say to you,
>   It shall be more tolerable for Tyre and Sidon
>   At the day of judgment
>   Than for you!

> And as for you, Capernaum, shalt though be exalted into
>   heaven?
> Thou shalt be brought down to hell!
>   For if the mighty works which have been done in you
>   Had been done in Sodom,
>   It would have remained until this day.
> But I say to you,
>   It shall be more tolerable for the land of Sodom
>   At the day of judgment
>   Than for you! (11:21–24)

The parallel treatment of these three Galilean cities, all of which face a terrible fate on the day of judgment for their failure to repent in the face of the mighty works that had been done in them, does not prepare us for the exceptional role that one of the three plays in the gospel stories of Jesus. All four gospels feature the city of Capernaum and give scant attention to the other two places which one would judge from the words of Jesus were the beneficiaries of his preaching and healing ministry no less than Capernaum.

The gospels, of course, tell the story of Jesus from the theological perspective of the mission to the Gentiles. In even the most Jewish of the four, the risen Jesus commands the eleven disciples to go and "make disciples of all the Gentiles" (Mt 28:19).

Indeed it is to the text of this gospel that we must go in our search for an answer to the question of how the city of Capernaum has come to play such a dominating role in the gospel story.

But first it is important for us to situate in our mind's eye the location of Capernaum in relation to other points of interest in the early church, especially the city of Damascus which lies to the northeast.

The Lake of Galilee is a great expanse of water fed by the Jordan River, which empties into the lake at its northern estuary and continues from the southern extremity, wending its way through the great Jordan valley until it finally empties into the

Dead Sea. Capernaum is situated at the northern end of the lake and west of the Jordan estuary. Here it occupies a prominent position at the crossroads of both land and sea routes leading north and east from Galilee.

The main road north from Judea and southern Galilee skirted the western coast of the lake until it reached a point just west of Capernaum. There it divided. One could continue north by ascending up the river bed of Nahal Korazim by way of the village and synagogue of Korazim (following the spelling of modern topography). One would then cross the Jordan over the B'noth-Ya'agor bridge and proceed eastward through Gualanitis (Golan) to Damascus. Or one could follow the eastern branch of this road at Capernaum and proceed along the northern coast of the Lake of Galilee leaving the port of Capernaum on the immediate right and thus in a short time reach the Jordan estuary. The river was crossed about one mile above the estuary via the ford at Beth-Saida (Bethsaida), which in the first century served as the capital of Philip the tetrarch of Gualanitis, Iturea, and Trachonitis. From Beth-Saida this road turned northward until it joined the Qu neitra-Damascus highway.[9]

As a port Capernaum was favorably located in relation to excellent fishing grounds near the Jordan estuary, and from Capernaum people had easy access by boat to Tiberias and about thirty other fishing villages all around the Lake of Galilee.[10] All in all Capernaum was well situated as a base for the disciples when they undertook, as in time they certainly did, the making of new disciples in areas north and east of Galilee. At any rate, however it happened, by the time the evangelist Matthew undertook to compose his gospel, Capernaum had become an important city in the salvation history of the Gentile church.

It is clear that the evangelist Matthew composed his gospel while standing in the tradition of an early Chrisitan mission that came originally out of northern Galilee. He takes as his *key text,* compositionally speaking, a text from Isaiah. In this text a passage which makes no reference to Capernaum is interpreted in a way that nonetheless makes Capernaum a part of God's plan of salvation for the Gentiles.[11] According to the Hebrew-Masoretic text, this passage from Isaiah reads:

> In the former time he brought into contempt the land of
> Zebulun and the land of Naphtali; but in the latter time
> he hath made it glorious, by the way of the sea, beyond
> the Jordan, Galilee of the Gentiles. The people that
> walked in darkness there have seen a great light: they
> that dwelt in the land of the shadow of death, upon
> them hath the light shined (9:1–2).

The Greek Septuagint version of this text in Matthew is
shortened and slightly modified:

> The land of Zebulun and the land of Naphtali, by the
> way of the sea, beyond the Jordan, Galilee of the Gen-
> tiles. The people that sat in darkness saw a great light;
> and to them that sat in the region and shadow of death,
> upon them hath the light shined.

The evangelist believes that the way to understand this text
is to realize that when the prophet Isaiah writes "by the way of
the sea," he is referring to the seacoast of the Lake of Galilee.
This we know because in the preceding verses Matthew notes
that in leaving Nazareth and coming to dwell in Capernaum *by
the sea* in the regions of Zebulun and Naphtali, Jesus did so in
order that the word of Isaiah the prophet might be fulfilled (4:13–
14).

Thus, Capernaum is important because, situated on the
coast of the Lake of Galilee, it can be interpreted as being "by the
way of the sea." Since there is nothing in the text of Isaiah that
refers to Capernaum, one must presume that Capernaum was in
some unexpressed way important to the evangelist. According to
the words of Jesus, Capernaum is notable as one of three cities
doomed for destruction because of its negative response to his
ministry. What then has happened to reverse this judgment of
Jesus so that in the gospel stories of God's salvation Capernaum
plays such a positive and important role?

One might say that there is no mystery, since we know that Jesus had a ministry in Capernaum, and since Capernaum was a city on the coast of the Lake of Galilee, it was natural for the evangelist to see Jesus' going to Capernaum as a fulfillment of the prophecy of Isaiah. However, it is equally clear that Jesus also had a ministry in other Galilean cities and villages, including significant evangelistic efforts in Chorazim and Bethsaida, and yet little or nothing is said about these ministries. Clearly a selective process has taken place which calls for an explanation.

Something very important concerning Capernaum must have taken place in order to account for its prominence in the gospel story. The evangelist has made this city the turning point in the whole development of Jesus' ministry. Following his baptism in the Jordan and his return to Nazareth in Galilee, Capernaum is the next place of importance. Jesus goes to Nazareth but nothing much of importance happens there. He goes immediately then to Capernaum where the first thing he does is to call Peter and his brother Andrew as well as James and John. He calls them from their fishing duties as his first disciples. Capernaum is the place where Jesus inaugurates his public ministry by calling disciples, three of whom, Peter, James, and John, will be with him at most of the high moments throughout his ministry. When compared to the rest of the twelve, these disciples, and especially Peter, clearly dominate the Jesus tradition that the evangelist will use in composing his gospel.

The best way to explain this selectivity is to recognize that the story of Jesus is being told from a particular perspective, i.e. that of the evangelist, or, better, that of the churches for which he is writing his gospel. The best way to explain this selectivity of emphasizing Capernaum and certain of the twelve is that Capernaum and some or all of those first disciples called by Jesus were singularly important in the history of the evangelist's church.

This is not to say that the story of Jesus has been falsified. Rather it is to say that the gospels grow out of an exegetical tradition. We make the best sense of this selectivity by positing that Jesus himself inaugurated this exegetical tradition through his reading of Isaiah. Since Isaiah was important to Jesus, Isaiah was important for his early disciples. The early Christians living on the coast of the Lake of Galilee, including any living in Capernaum, would have been the first to understand and appreciate this Matthean hermeneutical development within the Jesus-school Isaianic exegetical tradition. How are we to envision this? Our analysis suggests that this exegetical tradition developed in the hands of a Christian preacher in the city of Capernaum who interpreted the text of Isaiah to apply to the city in which he was preaching. "We here in this place have seen a great light." It would appear that in some such way the text of Isaiah has come to be seen in relationship to the history of the readers for whom the evangelist is writing.

Capernaum is one of many places frequented by Jesus. But this place, this particular place, because of its topographical importance, so well situated as a base for evangelistic outreach with good road and water connections, especially between Galilee and Damascus, becomes very important to the mission that moves from Galilee toward Damascus. Capernaum is the only city Jesus is known to have frequented that is situated on the seacoast made important by the prophecy of Isaiah, and which also served travelers on their way from Jerusalem to Damascus. Capernaum was a chief port of entry for travelers from southern Syria (including Damascus) into Galilee and points south (including Jerusalem). At the same time, and for similar reasons, it was the most suitable northern base for Christian missionary activity, moving out of Galilee into southern Syria. We know that Paul's persecution of Christians took him to Damascus, and that if he ever passed through Galilee on the way he would have passed by or very near to Capernaum.

The whole of this early church history makes sense if Peter was important in an early Christian mission going forth from Galilee into southern Syria and if this mission was sponsored by the church that Paul had been persecuting and from which he received the tradition he passed on to others after his conversion. This possibility would not have precluded Peter's spending periods of time in Jerusalem, and giving leadership to the twelve from that center.

PAUL'S RELATIONSHIP TO PETER

Looking at the matter in this way makes it possible for us to say that Paul entered into a partnership with Peter in principle the day he began preaching the faith of the church that he once ravished (Gal 1:23). There is nothing intrinsically implausible or improbable in this way of interpreting the evidence. It certainly helps us to understand how it was possible for Paul to visit Peter in Jerusalem and to remain with him for fifteen days.

It is altogether likely that each knew a good deal about the other long before they met in Jerusalem. And it is not unlikely that there had been some communication between them during the period Paul was preaching the gospel prior to his visit to Jerusalem to visit Peter. The visit itself almost certainly would have required some prior communication between them as well as some kind of pre-understanding.

Paul's decision to preach in Cilicia and points further west would have provided the occasion for him to visit Peter in Jerusalem and for him to reach a firm apostolic understanding with that apostle to whom the risen Christ, according to the tradition he had received, had indeed appeared first. Thereafter, wherever Paul went he passed on the tradition he had received from the mission Peter had organized and inspired.

I delivered to you first of all that which also I received: That Christ died for our sins according to the scriptures (Is 53); and that he was buried; and that he hath been raised on the third day according to the scriptures (Hos 6:2, Jon 2:1); and that he appeared to Cephas; then to the twelve; then he appeared to about five hundred brethren at the same time, of whom the majority abide with us until this day, but some have fallen asleep; then he appeared to James; then to all the apostles (1 Cor 15:3–7).

To this litany of what he had received which now he passes on to the Corinthians, Paul adds pertinent items from his own history with fitting theological and interpretative comments:

> And, last of all, as to one born out of due time he
> appeared also to me. For I am the least of the apostles,
> one who is not [even] worthy to be called an apostle,
> because I persecuted the church of God. But by the grace
> of God I am what I am, and his grace which I have
> received has not been without effect; on the contrary
> (because of the effect of God's grace) I labored more
> abundantly than all of them (i.e. the other apostles): yet
> not I but the grace of God which was with me. Whether
> it be I or they, so we preach, and so ye believed (8-11).

This tradition that Paul passes on, and which represents
Peter as the first to whom the risen Christ appeared, raises interesting questions. The gospel of Matthew, for example, preserves
a tradition according to which Jesus after his resurrection first
appeared to Mary Magdalene and the other Mary. It is argued
that Paul passes on a kerygma that must have the value of legal
testimony, and that since women's testimony was unacceptable
in Jewish courts, it was omitted altogether in kerygmatic pas-
sages, so that it would be wrong to argue that the tradition Paul
passes on conflicts with that from Matthew. In any case, it is clear
that Paul is passing on a pro-Petrine tradition, i.e. a tradition that
developed within a church in which it was remembered that the
risen Lord first appeared to Peter. That apostle to whom the risen
Christ was believed to have first appeared would have had a special place in post-resurrection churches. It is also important to
note that in Paul's version of this tradition Christ's appearance
to him, coming at the end of the series, "last of all," creates a
series which begins with Peter and ends with Paul. According to
Paul's version this is a closed canon of resurrection appearances.
It runs the gamut of apostolic authority—from Peter to Paul.
Paul is least of all, because he persecuted the church of God. But
he is also first because where sin doth abound there doth grace
much more abound. Similarly Paul can claim to have labored
more than any of the apostles, which would have included Peter.
So the last shall be first—whether by one's own labor in the gospel, or by God's grace.

Paul passed on a tradition that had developed in a church in which there was already present an incipient Petrine primacy. But his churches received this tradition from him within an overall theological framework which bespoke apostolic mutuality between the first of the twelve and the apostle to the Gentiles. Was this simply Paul's construction, or did it represent a bona fide apostolic agreement that had been reached between Peter and Paul before or during that fifteen day meeting in Jerusalem?

It must have represented an implicit apostolic quid-pro-quo whether consciously recognized or not. In any case no one can deny the facts: Paul passed on a pro-Petrine if not an implicit Petrine-primacy tradition and Peter supported Paul's right to head the apostolate to the Gentiles. Of course this understanding was not officially ratified by the pillars of the church in Jerusalem until fourteen years later when Paul returned to Jerusalem, and lay before those who had been apostles before him the gospel he had been preaching to the Gentiles.

It has been argued that the Jerusalem conference was only possible because Peter was willing to arrange it at Paul's request, and for the sake of the gospel.[12] According to this argument, the fundamental theological agreement reached between Peter and Paul during their fifteen day visit fourteen years before the apostolic conference (Gal 2:1–10), tested by fourteen years of missionary work by Paul and his associates, provided the essential components for the successful outcome of the apostolic conference. The agreement of the Jerusalem apostles to ratify the longstanding understanding between Peter and Paul, which issued in the decision to make each of them the heads of two separate but concordant missions, is the apostolic *magna charta* of the holy catholic church, reaffirmed martyrologically by signatures made in blood by these two chief apostles during the Neronian persecution. Paul gives his readers an eyewitness report of what actually happened at this historic conference. It is one of the most remarkable statements in the New Testament:

> When they (i.e. the pillars of the church in Jerusalem) saw that I had been entrusted with the gospel of the uncircumcision, even as Peter with the gospel of the circumcision (for he that wrought for Peter unto the apos-

tleship of the circumcision wrought for me also unto the Gentiles); and when they perceived the grace that was given unto me, James and Cephas and John, they who were reputed to be pillars, gave to me and Barnabas the right hands of fellowship, that we should go unto the Gentiles, and they unto the circumcision (Gal 2:7-9).

This dual leadership of the historical apostolate helps explain why the New Testament writings feature Peter and Paul. But the subsequent concordant martyrdom of these two apostolic heads is no less essential to the historical development that eventually led to the formation of the New Testament canon.[13]

There is a solid New Testament foundation for the recognition of Irenaeus that the founding and building up of the church in Rome by "the two most glorious (i.e. martyred) apostles Peter and Paul (*Ag Her* 3.3.2)" provide the holy catholic church with an essential touchstone in history for the combating of heresy. That which is not in harmony with the concordant apostolic witness of Peter and Paul sealed in blood and witnessed to in the scriptures which have been normed by this apostolic history and faith is not catholic, and cannot be accepted as being faithful to the primitive *regula,* i.e. the "truth of the gospel,"[14] by which these two apostles had agreed to norm their faith and practice (Gal 2:11-21).

Tertullian correctly saw that the norm by which the issue between Peter and Paul at Antioch was finally settled was in fact a primitive apostolic understanding based upon a theological agreement to which both Peter and Paul subscribed.[15] He understood this *regula* to have been laid down for the church by the apostles at the Jerusalem conference of Galatians 2:1-10. Our analysis leads to the conclusion that this apostolic conference was preceded by a less publicized and in some sense preparatory meeting, a meeting that had taken place between Peter and Paul in the same city fourteen years earlier (1:18).

In his first letter to the church at Corinth Paul addresses the problem of party spirit in that church and specifically refers to four parties, i.e. those who say "we belong to Paul," those who say "we belong to Apollos," those who say, "we belong to

Cephas," and those who say "we belong to Christ" (1 Cor 1:12). While Paul does not criticize Peter for contributing to this divisiveness, it is clear from the fact that there were members of the Corinthian church who said, "We belong to Cephas," that there was a basis for tension between Peter and Paul over the way in which their respective adherents behaved toward one another. Just how serious this tension may have been we do not know. There is no reference in any other letter of Paul to a "Cephas party." In Paul's second letter to the church at Corinth he is at pains to criticize certain opponents at Corinth who questioned his apostolic authority and worked against him. The depth of Paul's feeling about the challenge this opposition represented to his apostleship may be measured by his use of sarcasm in referring to them derogatorily as "super-apostles." While there is no way these "super-apostles" in 2 Corinthians can be identified with any degree of certainty as adherents of the "Cephas party" in 1 Corinthians, neither can one absolutely rule out the possibility that Paul's opponents in 2 Corinthians may have stood in some meaningful, even if undefinable, relationship to this party.

To the degree that we allow for the possibility that Paul's opponents in 2 Corinthians are related to the Cephas party mentioned in 1 Corinthians, the case for serious tension between Peter and Paul in the period following the apostolic conference in Jerusalem is strengthened. Certainly the incident that Paul relates in Galatians 2 concerning the confrontation he had with Peter over the issue of table fellowship between Gentile and Jewish Christians in Antioch serves to underscore the undeniable fact that these two apostles could differ strongly over very important issues. However, such disagreements in turn serve to underscore how firm was the bond that united them. The more we make room for post-conciliar tension, and the greater the place we give to this tension, the more we recognize the need for pre-conciliar solidarity to account for the eventual outcome. For if there is one thing that is certain in church history it is that in spite of any pig-headedness on the part of either or both of these great apostles, they did stand together on the fundamental theological basis of the faith, i.e. God's redemptive, sacrificial, and atoning love for sinners and all else that is entailed in the good news of justification by faith (2:15–21).

THE PRE-PAULINE TRADITION CONCERNING THE LORD'S SUPPER

Finally, in answer to the question "By what authority does the apostle to the Gentiles assure the Corinthian church that the tradition concerning the Lord's supper he had received, and had in turn passed on to them, originated with Jesus himself?" we answer, "by the authority of those who were apostles before him." And if it be asked "Did Paul have the opportunity to discuss the form, content, and credibility of this tradition with those apostles who were eyewitnesses to what actually happened in Jerusalem on the night when Jesus was delivered up?" the answer is most assuredly "Yes."

First he could, and presumably did, discuss such matters with Peter, who, according to the gospels (Mt 26:17-30 and parallels), was present there in Jerusalem that night in the very room where Jesus took bread and broke it. Second, Paul had further opportunity to discuss such matters with John as well as with Peter fourteen years later during the Jerusalem conference, if by that time he still had any questions. Paul's subsequent assurance to his readers in Corinth that he was passing on to them a tradition that he had received suggests that this tradition is handed on to us in the scriptures as tradition that comes not only with the authority of the apostle Paul but with that of those apostles Paul knew who had themselves been eyewitnesses to the event. We cannot be certain of this point. But it appears to us to be intrinsically probable in the light of the considerations to which attention has been brought in this essay.

The import of this conclusion is far-reaching. According to a pre-Pauline tradition "Christ died for our sins according to the scriptures" (1 Cor 15:3). Since Isaiah 53 is the only scripture theologians can supply to explain the meaning of the tradition Paul is passing on, we must be open to the conclusion that this passage in the book of Isaiah was important for Jesus. The evidence of his words preserved in Matthew 20:25–28 (and Mk 10:42–45), where the Son of Man gives his life as a ransom for many, argues for this conclusion.

It would follow in this case that for Jesus to speak as he spoke and to act as he acted on the night he was delivered up would have been for him to have taken a crucial step in instituting the church. And a church so instituted would be a church which in a central way would live out of the mystery of this eucharist. In other words it would be a martyrological church living out of the vicarious and atoning sacrifice of Jesus. The concordant martyrdom of the two chief apostles Peter and Paul in Rome would be inspired by the definitive faith that mysteriously comes to expression in the eyewitness tradition concerning this institutional act, and, as a rite, it would be central in the life and faith of that holy Catholic church within whose divine economy it would be the vocation of the church in Rome to represent the concordant witness of the chief apostles Peter and Paul, and to counsel with all churches which wish to remain faithful to that earliest apostolic witness: "In the night he was delivered up, he took bread. . . ." That is to say, words and deeds, as well as the death and resurrection of Jesus Christ, would be normative for the church in relationship to this central rite as the specification by our Lord of how the concord between the law and the prophets and the covenant that was coming into being through his death and resurrection was to be understood and lived out—a rite in which the fulfillment of the law and prophets is celebrated, the redeeming benefits of the atoning sacrifice of Christ are appropriated by faith, and the fruits of the Spirit that flow from the new covenant are shared by the participants.

CONCLUSION

The New Testament evidence indicates that there was a real partnership among the apostles, particularly between Peter and Paul. This partnership may well have allowed for an authority of Peter which expresses itself in guarding and strengthening the *koinōnia* of faith of all the apostles and in his being chief shepherd, while at the same time it allowed for an authority of Paul which expresses itself in charismatic foresight and theological depth. But to show what the partnership between Peter and Paul allowed by way of distinctive contributions from each to their apostolic leadership in founding and building up the church of Rome (*Ag Her* 3.3.3) would carry us into a discussion that goes beyond the limited purpose of this study. Our purpose has been to show that Irenaeus' perception of the church of Rome as a church which was founded and built up by Peter and Paul is a perception that is fully consonant with an historical analysis of Christian beginnings based upon the evidence made available to us in the individual books of the New Testament, taken together with a critical understanding of the formation of the New Testament canon within the context of early church history.

Chapter Three

PETER AND PAUL
IN THE THEOLOGIES
OF IRENAEUS AND TERTULLIAN

The most important early patristic texts which speak of the martyrdom of Peter, and his role in the foundation of the church of Rome (1 Clement, the Letter of Ignatius of Antioch to the Romans and the Letter of Bishop Dionysius of Corinth to the bishop of Rome) do not speak about Peter alone.[1] Paul is always joined with Peter. The two are associated as apostles, martyrs and the founders of the church of Rome.[2] The two most prominent theologians of the second century, Irenaeus and Tertullian, continue this early tradition. In the following pages I investigate in their works the theological significance of the joint role of Peter and Paul.

IRENAEUS

The Agreement of Peter and Paul

In order to prove the truth of the church's teaching in his own time, Irenaeus extols its identity with the preaching of the apostles. In this context Peter and Paul are often mentioned together. Paul can be mentioned before Peter, but, following historical order, Peter is almost always mentioned before Paul.[3] Irenaeus' favorite formula is: "Peter and Paul and the other apostles."[4] These two together represent all the other apostles and disciples of Jesus; they are the apostles par excellence, even though their testimony is complemented by that of the other apostles, in particular John and James (*Ag Her* 1.16.3; 3.12.15). Both Peter and Paul possess the full knowledge *(gnōsis)* of the mystery (1.13.6), and so their agreement is of crucial importance for exposing the errors of the various heresies. This needs to be shown in more detail.

Both Peter and Paul testify to the unity of the two Testaments which is the very basis of Irenaeus' theological synthesis. If the Valentinians do not admit the prophetic message about Christ, they should be consistent and refuse to believe that "Peter and Paul and the other apostles announced the truth" (4.35.2), since their teaching agrees with that of the prophets.[5] The Marcionites who claim that Paul alone knows the truth

> are proved wrong by Paul himself: one and the same God (the God of the Old Testament who is also the Father of Jesus Christ) worked in Peter for the apostolate of the circumcised and worked in him (Paul) for the Gentiles (3.13.1).

Irenaeus sees the basis for the agreement between Peter and Paul in the identity of the revelation they received as it becomes manifest in the close correspondence between Galatians 1:1, 16 and Matthew 16:17. He asks a rhetorical question: could the twelve apostles and the seventy disciples who were sent by the Lord to preach all be ignorant of the truth? Then he quickly comes to the decisive issue:

> Or how could Peter not know [the truth], Peter to whom the Lord testified that he received a revelation not from flesh and blood but from the Father in heaven (cf. Mt 16:17)? Therefore, just as Paul [became] apostle not by men or through human mediation, but through Jesus Christ and God the Father (Gal 1:1) [in the same way Peter and the other apostles have also come to know the Father and the Son], the Son leading them to the Father and the Father revealing them the Son (3.13.2; cf. Mt 11:25–27 and Gal 1:12,16).[6]

Irenaeus sees a parallelism between Galatians 1:1, 12, 16 and Matthew 11:25–27; 16:17, and he makes full use of it in order to point out that Paul and Peter (who stands also for the other apostles) received the same revelation. In both cases the ultimate source of knowledge is the Father, not a human being, and this knowledge comes to them directly rather than through a human intermediary. In both cases there is a dialectic relationship between the revealing activity of the Father and the Son. Both are simultaneously subjects and objects of revelation: the Father revealing the Son and the Son leading the apostles to the Father. The identity of the revelation to the two apostles is crucial for Irenaeus' argument against the Marcionites. Both Peter and Paul came to know one and the same God, the Father of Jesus Christ, besides whom there is no other god. This has been the main point of 3.15.1–3.

Upon closer examination the scriptural background of Irenaeus' text extends beyond a fusion of Matthew 11:25–27; 16:17 and Galatians 1:1, 12, 16. The expression "the Son leading them to the Father" ("adducente eos ad Patrem") echoes both 1 Peter 3:18 ("Christ suffered once for sins, the just one for the unjust that he might lead you to God . . .") and the Johannine theme of Christ on earth showing us the Father and promising to take us to the Father after his passing over to him (Jn 14). Thus for Irenaeus the revealing activity of Christ is not restricted to the appearances of the risen one as is the case for Paul in Galatians 1. It includes his whole earthly life, his death on the cross and his resurrection. So Irenaeus imposes the pattern of Matthew 11:25–27; 16:17 combined with 1 Peter 3:18 and John 14 on Galatians 1:1, 12, 16, rather than imposing the pattern of Galatians on the other texts. The emphasis is then not only on the same one God, but also on the incarnate Son on earth. This shows that Irenaeus anticipates here the emphasis of the next section beginning in 3.16.1. In arguing against the gnostics, he will use there again the testimony of Peter to prove that Jesus and the Christ, Jesus and the Son of God, did not separate from each other in the passion. Jesus Christ, the Son of God himself, suffered and died for us (3.18.4). Peter's confession also supports the virginal conception of Jesus: for Irenaeus, as for many other church fathers, Jesus could not be the Son of God if he had been engendered by Joseph. Peter's testimony is mentioned first and is followed by that of John, Matthew and Paul (3.21.3–10). We begin to see now the importance Irenaeus attributes to the identity of the revelation given to Peter and to Paul. In this way he assures that the Christ of Paul cannot be interpreted in a gnostic way. The risen Christ revealed to Paul may not be separated from the earthly Jesus revealed to Peter as the Son of God. They are one and the same. Thus, in Irenaeus' theology the identity of the revelation to the two chief apostles serves to guarantee not only the harmony of the two Testaments and the doctrine of the one God but also the reality of the incarnation and the passion of the Son of God.[7]

Another important issue for which the joint testimony of Peter and Paul is crucially important for Irenaeus is the authenticity of the three synoptic gospels:

Matthew among the Hebrews issued a written form of the gospel in their own language, while Peter and Paul were preaching the gospel in Rome and founding the Church *(themeliountōn tēn ekklēsian).* After their death *(exodos)* Mark, the disciple and interpreter of Peter, also handed down to us in writing what Peter had preached. Luke also, the follower of Paul, recorded in a book the gospel as it was preached by him. Finally John, the disciple of the Lord, who had also lain on his breast, himself published the gospel, while he was residing at Ephesus in Asia.[8]

We easily understand why the gospels of Mark and Luke need to be legitimized by the authority of Peter and Paul: their own authors cannot provide a guarantee since neither of them is an apostle. Moreover, the tradition of the historical link between the two gospels and the two apostles must have been familiar to Irenaeus. But relating the composition of Matthew among the Hebrews with the preaching and the church-founding activity of

Peter and Paul in Rome appears rather artificial. It seems that Irenaeus himself creates this tenuous link in order to extend the guarantee of Peter and Paul also to the gospel of Matthew. However, if we accept Farmer's reconstruction of the early development of the Roman canon, we can find the reason why Irenaeus invokes the authority of Peter and Paul to cover all the three synoptic gospels. At the time when Polycarp visited Anicetus in Rome, the gospels of Matthew, Mark and Luke were already in the possession of the Roman church, but the fourth gospel was included in the Roman canon only after Polycarp's conference with Anicetus.[9] If this is true, then Irenaeus, who may have been in Rome at the time of this historic meeting in 154 A.D., and who certainly went to Rome in 177, reflected in his book the consciousness of the Roman church: at that time Rome considered all the three synoptics as her own gospels and naturally linked them to Peter and Paul. As the church of Rome saw her own guarantee in that she was founded by Peter and Paul, she attributed the same guarantors to the three gospels which she had traditionally considered as her own.

Peter and Paul and the Authority of the Church of Rome

How then is the theological importance of the church of Rome connected with Peter and Paul in Irenaeus' mind? After Irenaeus explains the general principle that the tradition of the apostles can be found everywhere in every church in which one is able to enumerate the successors of the apostles up to the present, he continues:

> But since it would be very long in such a volume as this to enumerate the successions of all the churches, I can, by pointing out the tradition which that very great, oldest, and well-known church, founded and established at Rome by those two most glorious apostles Peter and Paul, received from the apostles, and the faith she has announced to men, which comes down to us through the successions of bishops, put to shame all of those who

in any way, either through wicked self-conceit, or through vainglory, or through blind and evil opinion, gather as they should not *(praeterquam oportet colligunt)*. For every church, that is, the faithful from everywhere, must be in harmony with this church because of its most excellent origin, in which (church) the tradition coming from the apostles has always been preserved for the faithful from everywhere *(ad hanc enim Ecclesiam propter potentiorem principalitatem necesse est omnem convenire Ecclesiam, hoc est eos qui sunt undique fideles, in qua semper ab his qui sunt undique conservata est ea quae est ab apostolis traditio).*

After the blessed apostles had founded and built up the church *(themeliōsantes . . . kai oikodomēsantes . . . tēn ekklēsian),* they handed over the ministry of the episcopate to Linus.[10]

Then Irenaeus enumerates the succession of bishops up to Eleutherus. The most controversial part of the text is the sentence I quote fully in Latin. I cannot review here all the interpretations this text has elicited throughout the centuries. While keeping in mind the most important trends of interpretation, I will outline mine which takes its starting point from the notes of the critical edition by Rousseau and Doutreleau and from the excellent articles of E. Lanne.[11] The understanding of the passage depends on the meaning of a few key terms.

"Omnem ecclesiam"

The words *omnem ecclesiam* have often been interpreted in a restrictive sense: it would mean only the church of Lyons and the churches of the west founded by Rome. However, the division of Christianity into a western and eastern half took place after the second century. Projecting it into the time of Irenaeus would be an anachronism. Moreover, through his personal background Irenaeus serves as a bridge between the churches of Asia Minor and those of the west. Wherever else he uses the term *pasa ekklēsia,* he means every local church everywhere in the world.

There is no reason, then, to attribute a restrictive meaning to the term in this passage.

"Propter potentiorem principalitatem"

The meaning of the phrase *propter potentiorem principalitatem* is crucial for understanding the text. *Principalitas* or the adjective *principalis* has a variety of meanings in *Against Heresies* depending on the context. It may be the translation of *authentia:* sovereignty, a technical term in gnostic theology,[12] of *hēgemonikon:* principal, ruling, leading,[13] or *archē:* origin, or *archaion:* original, ancient,[14] and of the verb *prōteuein:* to be first in the transcendent sense of being the highest and all-determining principle.[15]

"Enim"

The term *enim (gar)*, "for," introduces the next sentence as the reason for what has been said beforehand. As Rousseau and Doutreleau have shown, this explicative use of *enim (gar)* is typical of Irenaeus.[16] If this is true, the phrase "propter potentiorem principalitatem" must refer to and further explain what was said in the previous sentence about the founding of the church of Rome by the two glorious apostles Peter and Paul. Thus the original Greek phrase may have been *dia tēn hikanōteran archēn*[17] which would be translated "because of its most (or more) excellent origin."

This interpretation from the immediate context is confirmed from the line of reasoning of the entire work, *Against Heresies*. Irenaeus' argument against all the heretics is based on the normative character of the apostolic origin of the churches. All heresies came about after the church had already been established. They are all *"adinventiones,"* later human inventions.[18] They take their origins *(tas archas)* from the father of the heresy, while the churches derive their succession from the apostles.[19] The heretics stay away "from the original succession" *("a principali successione")* which consists in the sequence Lord–apostles–churches; the Lord delivered the true doctrine to the apostles, the apostles to the churches, and in the churches it survived intact up to this very day through the succession of presbyter-bishops.[20] Therefore the true tradition is always the *"vetus traditio,"* *hē archaia paradosis,* "the original tradition" that can be traced back to the apostles.[21]

"In qua"

The term *in qua* could refer grammatically either to *omnem ecclesiam* or to *ad hanc . . . ecclesiam.* However, Irenaeus' line of thought excludes the former. The whole section aims at putting to shame those who "gather as they should not" by pointing out that they ought to agree with the church of Rome. If *in qua* referred to all the churches, it would contravene Irenaeus' argument.

If the Latin text is a correct reading of the original Greek, *in qua semper ab his qui sunt undique conservata est ea quae est ab apostolis traditio* must be translated in these or similar terms: "in which the tradition coming from the apostles has always been preserved by the faithful from everywhere." The church of Rome would then serve as a representation of the universal church; the faithful flocking to Rome from everywhere in the world would present a cross-section of the church universal and they would provide a tangible proof that all the faithful preserve the apostolic tradition. We cannot exclude such an interpretation. Rome was indeed an international center where people (including Christians) converged from everywhere in the world. In this case, Irenaeus would state that all the churches must agree with the church of Rome because in her the apostolic tradition has been preserved by the faithful coming to Rome from every part of the world as pilgrims, visitors, settlers, etc. Such an interpretation, however, is unrelated to the context. Before and after the phrase in question Irenaeus insists on the apostolic origin of the church of Rome rather than on its being an international center for the faithful from every part of the world. Moreover, before and after the phrase in question, Irenaeus stresses the active role of Rome for the other churches. He mentions the faith "that she has announced to men."[22] In the next paragraph, when enumerating the succession of the bishops of Rome, Irenaeus describes the effects of "the most important letter of the church in Rome" to the rebellious Corinthians. The letter restored them to peace, renewed their faith and announced to them the tradition they had once received from the apostles.

If, however, we accept the reconstructed Greek text of Rousseau and Doutreleau, *en hē aei tois pantachōthen ephylachthē hē apo tōn apostolōn paradosis,* and accept a single mistake on the part of the Latin translator (mistaking *tois* for a dative of agent instead of understanding it as a dative of reference), the resulting meaning fits perfectly the context: "in which the tradition coming from the apostles has always been preserved for the faithful from everywhere." This somewhat lengthy explanation was necessary since none of the existing English translations of Irenaeus' works has, to my knowledge, adopted the emended text of Rousseau-Doutreleau.

Before we further specify the meaning of this text, we need to confront its traditional Catholic exegesis as best exemplified by Battifol and Ludwig.[23] In various ways both of them think that for Irenaeus the reason for the *potentior principalitas* of Rome is its foundation by Peter who is seen by Irenaeus in the light of Matthew 16:17–19. Both ignore the role Paul has played according to Irenaeus in the prominence of Rome. Reminiscences of Matthew 16:17 are certainly present in the last paragraph of the text: *oikodomēsantes . . . hoi makarioi . . . tēn ekklēsian* occur together in the New Testament only in Matthew 16:17–18. Their combined use by Irenaeus in a text that mentions Peter can hardly be a coincidence. The word *themeliōsantes,* however, reflects Pauline terminology: Romans 15:20, 1 Corinthians 3:10–11, Ephesians 2:20. The classic verb "to found" would be *hidryō* which Irenaeus uses only when he speaks about churches which were not founded by apostles. Whenever he writes about the church-founding activity of Peter and Paul, he uses the Pauline term *themelioō.* He also extends the Matthean epithet *makarios* to Paul.[24]

This interpretation of Matthean-Petrine and Pauline terminology and the joint appearance of Peter and Paul in the previous sentence (to which the sentence in question is linked by an explicative *enim, gar*) indicate that Peter alone, even if understood against the faint background of Matthew 16:17–19, cannot account for the *potentior principalitas* of the church of Rome. A second alternative seems much more probable. The joint activity of the two "most glorious apostles" Peter and Paul in Rome, their preaching to, founding and building up the church of Rome, is the most obvious ground for Rome's special position.

Moreover, as E. Lanne has shown convincingly, the adjective *gloriosissimis* suggests that Irenaeus considers their joint martyrdom as the definitive act of establishing the church of Rome in its unique function for the universal church. In what follows I will summarize Lanne's insights.[25] Since the apostles, in particular Peter and Paul, received revelation from the Son and the Father, they are perfect in knowledge, and so are their disciples by receiving knowledge from them. Yet they fulfill this perfect doctrine in their lives only when "imitating the master of martyrdom," only when they themselves become martyrs. For instance, Stephen "was stoned to death, and, in this manner, he fulfilled the perfect teaching" *(perfectam doctrinam adimplevit)* (3.12.13). We find in Irenaeus' thought many considerations which show that for him martyrdom is Christian perfection, and consequently (even though he does not make it explicit) also the bringing to perfection of apostleship and apostolic preaching. I will mention here only the most important reasons.

1.   Martyrdom is the highest manifestation of love and love is the most excellent charism in the church, even better than true gnosis which is the apostolic teaching (4.33.8–9).

2.   The prophets showed in their lives that those on whom the Spirit will rest and who obey the word of the Father and serve him with all their strength will be persecuted and killed by those opposing the truth. Thus martyrdom provides the highest credential for the teacher; it reveals that his teaching was inspired by the Holy Spirit. What he spoke was no mere human opinion, but God's teaching (3.12.13; 14.33.9–10).

3.   By conforming to the "master of martyrdom," the martyr makes him visible in his body. As "The Letter of the Martyrs of Gaul" (coming from the church community of Irenaeus)

explains, the fellow martyrs of Blandina, when looking at the suffering girl, "beheld with their outward eyes, in the form of their sister, him who was crucified for them" (Eus, *Eccl Hist* 5.1.41).

4. The Spirit strengthens the flesh of the martyr so that he conquers all suffering and becomes truly alive for God. After his death, then, the martyr does not disappear from the church. On the contrary, he is now in that perfect state in which the whole church will be at the end of time. The church "sends him ahead" ("praemittit") to the Father (4.33.9).

5. Irenaeus does not himself speak about the activity of the martyrs in the church after their death, but we may assume that he shares the views of Ignatius from whose letter to the Romans he quotes approvingly (5.28.40). Ignatius knows that he will be a truly credible Christian *(pistos)* only when the world sees him no more, just as Jesus Christ whose martyrdom he is going to imitate is more revealed now that he is in the Father than he was during his earthly life (*Rom* 3.2–3). If not allowed to become a martyr, Ignatius, once again, will be only a "voice" *(phōnē),* whereas, if he dies as a martyr, he will become "the word of God" *(logos theou)* (2.1). In other words, as a result of his martyrdom, Ignatius hopes to become so identified with the word of God that he himself, his very person, will manifest God's word.

When addressing the church of Rome, Ignatius compares himself to Peter and Paul:

> I don't give orders as Peter and Paul. They are apostles, I am a convict *(ekeinoi apostoloi, egō katakritos).* They are free men, I am still a slave *(ekeinoi eleutheroi, egō de mechri nyn doulos).* But if I suffer, I will become the freedman of Jesus Christ and in him I will rise to freedom (4.3).

In Ignatius' thought the apostles Peter and Paul are free men now as a result of their martyrdom. Therefore, the parallel predicate noun "apostles" must also refer to the present. Peter and Paul are apostles even now, at the time of Ignatius. It is likely, then, that in the first sentence the elliptical comparative clause "as Peter and Paul" may also be completed by a verb in the present, "as Peter and Paul do."

Let us draw now the conclusion that Ignatius merely implies. If Ignatius, who is no apostle but a bishop, will start his most effective witnessing activity only as a result of his martyrdom, how much more must Peter and Paul, who are apostles, be active in the present. Present in Rome, they remain the word of God for the church of Rome and for all the churches. We may assume that also for Irenaeus Peter and Paul are perfected as witnesses to God's word through their martyrdom, and their witness endures in and through the church of Rome up to the days of Irenaeus.

"Duobus"

Finally, we need to inquire into the meaning of the word *duobus* within the phrase: *a gloriosissimis duobus apostolis Petro et Paulo Romae fundatae et constitutae ecclesiae.* Lanne observes the word has a *"nuance d'insistance."*[26] In no other text in which Irenaeus mentions Peter and Paul together does he add the word "two" except here where he writes about the foundation of the church of Rome by the two martyr apostles. Recalling the theological importance of Peter and Paul in the whole work *Against Heresies,* we may explain this insistence by the fact that for Irenaeus Peter and Paul stand for all the apostles and they together guarantee the fullness of apostolic doctrine. Thus their joint founding of the church of Rome provides a unique fullness of apostolicity for this church.

How the agreement of the two martyr apostles confirms their witness and thereby enhances the importance of the church of their joint martyrdom is shown by the way Irenaeus discredits the teachings of the gnostics. He points out that the principle of witnessing by the prophets, by the Lord and by the apostles is important also for the heretics. They try to forge a link between their stories and the Lord's parables, the prophetic sayings and apostolic sermons "so that their concoction may not appear without a witness" (1.8.1). Moreover, Irenaeus hastens to show that their teachings are not only opposed to the testimony of the biblical witnesses, but they also disagree among themselves:

> Let us look now at the unstable opinion of these men: wherever there are two or three of them, they do not say the same things about the same matters, but rather contradict one another both in thought and in words (1.11.1).

The introduction to the second part of the first book of *Against Heresies* shows the context in which their disagreement should be viewed. It stands in direct opposition to the "one soul," to the "one and the same heart" and to the "one mouth" of the church which believes everywhere in the same way (1.10.2). "Wherever there are two or three of them" intends to show the contrast of the situation of the heretics and the situation of the disciples described in Matthew 18:20. Just as the agreement of two or three disciples manifests the unanimity of the faith of the church and thereby the almighty presence of Christ among them, the fact that not even two or three gnostics agree on a teaching proves that they do not have the faith of the church and therefore they cannot be true witnesses to it.

It seems, then, that in Irenaeus' mind the martyrdom of the *two* apostles Peter and Paul in Rome confirms the unique normative role of that church for the faith of the church universal. Their joint witness is sign and proof of the one apostolic faith which that church has received from them and still possesses.

The Church of Rome and the Easter Controversy from the Viewpoint of Irenaeus

The Easter controversy in the last decade of the second century provides for us some kind of a "test case" to study how Irenaeus understood the normative authority of the church of Rome. Bishop Victor of Rome threatened with excommunication the churches of Asia Minor for refusing to give up their tradition of celebrating Easter on the 14th day of Nisan according to the Jewish tradition rather than on Sunday as the church of Rome and most other churches were doing.[27]

Without discussing the details and the merits of the issue, I intend here only to investigate the attitude of Irenaeus as it contrasts with that of Victor and of Polycrates, the leader of the Asian bishops, who opposed Victor. It is difficult to assess the situation since Eusebius' own summary of the events does not quite correspond to what the quoted fragments of his sources say. We may assume, however, that there were two interrelated issues: the date of the celebration of Christ's resurrection on the one hand and the date and manner of abstinence and fasting on the other. The regional synods, especially the one held in Rome, decreed that the mystery of the Lord's resurrection must be celebrated only on Sunday *(Eccl Hist* 5.23.2–3), while Polycrates speaking in the name of the bishops of Asia Minor insisted that one must observe the "fourteenth of the Pascha." Whatever else this observance on the fourteenth meant, it certainly included abstinence from leavened bread according to Polycrates (5.23.6) and/or some preparatory fasting of different lengths and at variance with the Roman custom, according to Irenaeus (5.24.12–13). The latter seems to be the neuralgic point on which Victor and Polycrates clash: "Seven of my relatives were bishops, I am the eighth; and my relatives have always kept the day when the people abstained from leavened bread" (5.24.6), boasts Polycrates. He supports his position in the following way:

> We for our part keep the day scrupulously without addition or subtraction. For great luminaries rest also in Asia *(kai gar kata tēn Asian)* who shall rise again on the day of the Lord's advent (5.24.2).

These great luminaries are the apostle Philip (confused with Philip the evangelist of Acts 21:8) who sleeps in Hierapolis with his two daughters and John who leant back on the Lord's breast, priest, martyr and teacher, who rests in Ephesus. There are also some others, such as Polycarp of Smyrna, bishop and martyr, and Melito of Sardis who lived entirely in the Holy Spirit.

Since Polycrates introduces his argument by "also in Asia," we may surmise with E. Lanne that, by listing the tombs and presence of these apostles, bishops and martyrs, Polycrates intends to match a similar claim by Victor.[28] Judging from Polycrates' reply, Victor may have derived his authority for excommunicating entire churches not from any Petrine text of the New Testament but from the tombs and presence of the martyr apostles Peter and Paul in Rome. If this is true, then Irenaeus and Victor agree on the basis of the *potentior principalitas* for the church of Rome.

Even though Polycrates refuses to yield to Victor on the issue of the "fourteenth day," he acknowledges that he called together the bishops of Asia Minor at Victor's initiative: in his own words, "the bishops who are with me whom you yourself have deemed appropriate to be called together by me" (5.24.8). This suggests that the other synods held at the same time, such as the gathering of the bishops of Palestine, Pontus, Gaul, and Osroenes (5.23.3–4), were also convoked at the prompting of Victor. Thus Victor's activity reveals both an awareness of his authority to decide who belongs to the universal church but also a policy of collegial action, consulting with his brother bishops before making a decision.

It is obvious that both Polycrates and Victor are convinced that the observance or non-observance of the "fourteenth day" belongs to the rule of faith. Polycrates strikes a solemn tone as if he were defending his faith:

When blessed Polycarp paid a visit to Rome in Anicetus' time, though they had minor differences on other matters too, they at once made peace, having no desire to quarrel on this point. Anicetus could not persuade Polycarp not to keep the day, since he had always kept it with John the disciple of the Lord and the other apostles with whom he had been familiar; nor did Polycarp persuade Anicetus to keep it: Anicetus said that he must stick to the practice of the presbyters before him. Even though this was the state of affairs, they remained in communion with each other, and in church Anicetus made way for Polycarp to celebrate the eucharist—out of respect obviously. They parted company in peace, and the whole church was at peace, both those who kept the day and those who did not (5.24.16–17).

Irenaeus' position is clearly distanced from that of both Polycrates and Victor. In spite of his devotion to Polycarp whom he had known personally and in spite of his respect for John the apostle on whose authority the quartodeciman tradition relies, Irenaeus does not accept the binding character of that tradition. On the contrary, he sides with the Sunday tradition of Rome and of the majority of churches. Whether he considers the celebration of the resurrection only on Sunday as part of the rule of faith is not quite clear. But he certainly opposes the intransigent attitude of Victor who wants "to cut off entire churches of God" for observing a contrary tradition of ancient custom (5.24.11). Moreover, he does not see the differences in fasting as having any bearing on the rule of faith (5.24.13).[29]

We may now summarize our conclusions. For Irenaeus, Peter and Paul are the most important apostles and also represent all the others. Their complete agreement guarantees the truth of the church's preaching against all heresies. They also warrant, as a last instance, the authenticity of the three synoptic gospels. Although Irenaeus echoes Matthew 16:18, he never explicitly uses Matthew 16:18–19 to establish the prominence of Peter.

In Irenaeus' thought Peter appears to have the same dignity and importance as Paul, except for the fact that Peter is consistently mentioned before Paul. Their equal or near equal status derives from the fact that both received the same revelation from the Father and the Son.

The normativity of the church of Rome for all the other churches is not based on any Petrine text of the New Testament but rather on its joint foundation by the two most important martyr apostles Peter and Paul. This normativity concerns only "the one and the same faith" and allows for a plurality of local traditions. Nor does the *potentior principalitas* of the Roman church exempt the conduct of her bishop from criticism by his fellow bishops when the bishop of Rome attempts to impose on other churches a tradition which is not part of the rule of faith.

TERTULLIAN

The Agreement of Peter and Paul

Just as Irenaeus, so also Tertullian considers the doctrinal agreement of Peter and Paul crucially important for refuting heretics, in particular Marcion. He states repeatedly that Peter and Paul have the same faith and preach the same doctrine. They agree even on the matter of women's dress: both of them reject extravagance. They speak "by the same mouth because they are inspired by the same Spirit."[30]

Tertullian comments on Galatians 1–2 four times, once in *Prescription against Heretics* and three times in *Against Marcion.* His line of thought is almost the same in both works, but we find some change in his evaluation of the clash between Peter and Paul in Antioch. In both works Tertullian insists that the conflict between Paul on one side and Peter and "those with him" (*Pre* 23.1), "the other pillars" (*Marc* 4.3.3), on the other was a matter of *conversatio,* not *praedicatio,* "conduct," not "preaching" (*Pre* (*Pre* 23.10). The disagreement on conduct does not change the fact that Peter and "those with him" gave Paul their right hand, "the sign of agreement and unanimity." They did not divide the gospel "so that one would preach one gospel and the other another gospel, but rather that each of them would present the same gospel to a different audience, Peter to the circumcision and Paul to the Gentiles" (*Pre* 23.9). With regard to the disagreement in *conversatio,* in *Prescription against Heretics* Tertullian admits the possibility that Peter indeed may have committed a fault. Yet he hastens to add that it was a "fault of conduct rather than of preaching."[31] In *Against Marcion* he definitely takes the side of Peter. He reminds his readers that later Paul himself followed the example of Peter by becoming everything for everyone, Jew for the Jews, being under the law for those who were under it (cf. 1 Cor 9:19–22). He excuses Paul's criticism of Peter by recalling that Paul, at that time, was still "uneducated in the matters of grace" *(rudis in gratia)* and acted with the fervor of a neophyte (1.20.2–3; cf. also 4.3.3 and 5.3.6–8).

We notice also a shift in describing the relationship between Peter and Paul from *Prescription against Heretics* to *Against Marcion*. In the former work Paul seems to be equal to Peter. In the latter Tertullian subordinates Paul to Peter and the other apostles to the point of slightly misrepresenting the perspective of Galatians. According to Tertullian, Paul was "trembling" *(trepidus)* when going up to Jerusalem (1.20.2) "to get the patronage *(patrocinium)* of Peter and of the other apostles in order to confer with them about the rule of his gospel lest he had run in vain or would run in vain if he taught anything outside their rule of teaching *(citra formam illorum evangelizaret)*. . . . He wished to be approved and to be confirmed by them (*ab illis probari et constabiliri desiderarat)*" (5.3.1).[32]

Tertullian here simplifies Paul's complex attitude as it appears in the letter to the Galatians. He presents only the Paul who submits his gospel for scrutiny to Peter and the other apostles, and passes over in silence Paul's conviction that he received his gospel directly from God and is absolutely sure of its truth. This shift in favor of Peter to whom Paul must be subordinated reflects Tertullian's anti-Marcionite concern. The Marcionite interpretation of Paul may have convinced Tertullian that Paul needs to be integrated into a broader synthesis under the leading role of Peter and the other apostles whom Peter represents.

The Martyr Apostles Peter and Paul and the Church of Rome

We have seen that in Irenaeus the normativity of Rome is based on its foundation by the two martyr apostles Peter and Paul. This line of thought is further developed by the early Tertullian. In *Prescription against Heretics* Tertullian suggests to those who want to know more about their faith to visit the apostolic churches, that is, the churches founded by an apostle. If the student is close to Achaia, he can visit Corinth; if he is not far from Macedonia, he has Philippi; if he can travel to Asia, he should visit Ephesus; if he is close to Italy, he should go to Rome

(36.1–2). The following traits characterize all the apostolic churches:

> the very chairs of the apostles still preside in their places ... their original letters are still read, resounding the voice and making visible the face of each (36.1).

However, Tertullian mentions apostolic martyrdom only in connection with the founding of the church of Rome. He exclaims:

> How fortunate is this church into which the apostles poured forth all their teaching along with their blood *(cui totam doctrinam apostoli cum sanguine suo profuderunt),* where Peter is made equal to the suffering of the Lord, where Paul is rewarded by the death of John, from where the apostle John, after being immersed into boiling oil without suffering, is exiled onto an island *(ibid.* 3).

I think this is the strongest affirmation in early Christian literature of the link between apostolic martyrdom and church-founding. From this text it appears that for Tertullian church-founding meant primarily the preaching of all the doctrines by the apostles and the reception of the same by the church. This pouring into the church of all their teaching was strengthened by the pouring forth of their blood. One thinks instinctively of the ancient city-building ritual according to which the blood of a human victim had to be mixed with the mortar so that the walls of the city might become strong and indestructible. The pagan image may have helped Tertullian coin the phrase but the reality expressed is that of Christian faith. The blood of the apostles poured out in martyrdom leads to trust in the truth of their teaching *(Apol* 21.25). Through suffering their faith is tested and proved authentic just as gold and silver are proved in the fire *(Antidote* 7.4). The martyrs teach by their deeds more effectively than the pagan philosophers by their words. Their strength in suffering is the most effective teacher (*Apol* 50.14–16). The disciples (Tertullian may be thinking here primarily about Peter and Paul) have sown the Christian blood in Rome through Nero's savagery (*ibid.* 21.25). Indeed, "the blood of Christians is seed" (*ibid.* 50.13). It makes the church fertile and growing.

Does it contribute to the importance of the church of Rome in Tertullian's mind that Peter and Paul both died as martyrs there? Their common martyrdom raises both of them to a high dignity; both of them become guaranteed witnesses of the gospel. The particular fact that "Peter is made equal to Paul even in martyrdom" (*Pre* 24.4) corroborates Tertullian's argument against the heretics who reject Peter but extol Paul.

However, the text we quoted above suggests an added significance for the church of Rome on the ground that in Rome three apostles bore witness as martyrs, Peter, Paul and John. Tertullian makes much of the legal principle which is based on a particular version of Deuteronomy 19:15: "every word will stand on the testimony of three witnesses" (*Bapt* 6.2; *Pre* 22.6; *Marc* 3.9.4; 4.22.7; 5.12.9). He seems to know only this variant of the saying because he consistently omits "two or." He applies this saying primarily to God's word: "every word of God will stand on the testimony of three witnesses" (*Bapt* 6.2). For this reason Jesus takes only three disciples with him to the mountain: "not because the Lord rejected the others, but because every word will stand on the testimony of three witnesses" (*Pre* 22.6). By observing this injunction of the law, Jesus shows that he is the Christ of the creator God. Thus the unity of both Testaments and the unity of God are attested, and the Marcionites are proved wrong.

It is against this background that we venture an hypothesis: the principle of the three witnesses explains the appearance of John as confessor next to the martyr apostles Peter and Paul in *Prescription against Heretics* 36.3, where Tertullian intends to demonstrate the unique authority of the church of Rome. For Irenaeus the foundation of the church of Rome by the two martyr apostles Peter and Paul was sufficient to establish its normativity. Tertullian, working with the principle of three witnesses, had to introduce a third apostolic witness, the quasi-martyr John, in order to justify the unique position of Rome.[33] Rome alone, in the works of Tertullian, had the privilege of the joint foundation and martyrdom of Peter and Paul and the confession of faith of John the apostle. This is why Tertullian shifts from the declaratory enumerating the apostolic churches in 36.1–2 to an exclamatory "How fortunate is this church" in 36.3.[34]

However, my hypothesis does not imply that Tertullian invented the Roman sojourn and the boiling of John in hot oil. There may have been sources earlier than Tertullian that are now lost. Considering the unusual mobility of Christians in the empire, we cannot exclude the possibility that John indeed came to Rome. On the other hand, the genesis of the story could be explained simply by the presence of the Johannine writings in the church of Rome. Tertullian himself mentioned that the public reading of the apostles' letters made their voice resound and their faces be seen in the apostolic churches. We may assume that the continued reading of the Johannine writings in Rome made John present in the mind and imagination of the community. This may have given rise to the story of John's sojourn and confession of faith in Rome. As a legendary development the story is nonetheless based on a literary and theological truth: it is the apostle himself who speaks and bears witness to the word of God in the church through the public reading of his writings.

Beyond their teaching, their memory and the sacred books guaranteed by their authority, does Tertullian envision a personal presence and influence of Peter and Paul in the church of Rome? He certainly implies a permanent connection between Paul and the city of Rome. "Paul obtains birth in the city of Rome when he is reborn there through the generosity of martyrdom" (*Antidote* 15.3). His new birth not only allows the martyr to enter the kingdom of heaven but also associates him with the city where he suffered. Remarkably, however, Tertullian does not say anything about Peter's "birth" in the city of Rome. Nevertheless his statement about Paul makes him the first explicit witness to a developing belief which will affirm that the martyred apostles Peter and Paul are personally present and active in the church of Rome.[35]

The Unique Position of Peter in the Church Based on Matthew 16:18–19

In addition to the clearly perceptible shift toward subordinating Paul to Peter, and to associating John with Peter and Paul in order to strengthen the authority of the church of Rome, we find another new feature regarding the position of Peter in the works of Tertullian. Peter emerges alone, apart from Paul, serving as a foundation for the universal church.

Tertullian does not even mention the revelation made to Peter, an event so fundamental for Irenaeus. For Tertullian Peter's unique function in the universal church is based on Matthew 16:18–19. In *Prescription against Heretics* we find the first quotation of this text in the history of the church. Against the assertion of the gnostics that the apostles did not know all the teachings of Christ, Tertullian replies with a series of rhetorical questions very reminiscent of Irenaeus (*Ag Her* 3.13.1). He asks whether any sensible man would believe that those whom Christ has appointed as teachers, who were his inseparable companions, disciples and sharers in his life, could have been unaware of his teaching. In particular,

> Could anything be hidden from Peter, the one called the rock on which the church was to be built *(aedificandae ecclesiae petram dictum),* who received the keys of the kingdom of heaven and the power to loose and bind in heaven and on earth? Could anything be hidden from John, the beloved (disciple) of the Lord to whom alone the Lord pointed out in advance Judas, his traitor, and whom he entrusted to Mary as her son in his own place (22.4–5)?

As Ludwig correctly remarks, the abbreviated text of Matthew 16:18–19, which is quoted without any further explanation, suggests that the passage was well-known to Tertullian's audience, just as the short references from John 13:23, 25–26 and

19:26-27 reflect the knowledge of these texts in the church of Africa.[36]

Tertullian wonders why Jesus gave the name Peter to his disciple. If Jesus had picked *Petrus* (*petra* = rock) because of the vigor of the disciple's faith, many other materials equally solid as rock could have served equally well. So there had to be another reason. The disciple received the name "rock" because Christ himself is a "rock." Scripture indicates that Christ has been set up as the stone against which one stumbles, "the rock of scandal" (Is 8:14).

> He wanted to share lovingly with his dearest disciple a name taken from his own symbols *(de figuris suis)*. I think this was more appropriate than a name from among those that were not his own (*Marc* 4.13.6).

The new name given by Jesus to Peter symbolizes his role in God's plan. Peter's receiving the name "rock," which symbolizes the role of Jesus, suggests a close relationship between the two. In God's plan Peter the rock participates in the role of Jesus the rock.

It is also notable that the scriptural foundation for this relationship between Jesus and Peter is the Pauline text: 1 Corinthians 10:4: "The rock in fact was Christ *(Petra autem erat Christus)*." In *Against Marcion* we read, "Or because Christ is both rock and stone *(An quia et petra et lapis Christus)*" Thus Tertullian, the first to use Matthew 16:18-19 in Christian literature, was also the first to find the key for its christological interpretation in the ecclesiology of Paul. According to 1 Corinthians, even though it was the apostle Paul who laid the foundation for the church of Corinth, no mere man, not even an apostle, can be called the foundation of the church. There is no other foundation but Jesus Christ himself (cf. 1 Cor 3:10-11). Tertullian may have felt a tension between the ecclesiology of Matthew 16:18-19 and that of 1 Corinthians which led him—instinctively rather than through developing a philosophical theory—to imply a relationship of participation between Jesus and Peter.

What, then, does Tertullian mean by indicating that Peter participates in Christ as the rock? Peter is to serve as the foundation on which the church is to be built. In particular, Christ

> will set up all the ranks of his order from monogamous people upon him in the church *(super illum omnem gradum ordinis sui de monogamis erat collocaturus),*

declares the Montanist Tertullian (*Monog* 8.4).[37] However, one finds no reason to suppose that this is a Montanist teaching. It rather derives from Tertullian's Catholic heritage. Peter is the foundation of all church order, not only of bishops and deacons, but also of widows as listed in 1 Timothy 3:1–13; 5:9–10. All those who are part of the institution of Christ *(ordinis sui)* are built upon Peter (cf. *Monog* 11.4; *Chast* 13.4; 7.2–3). In the words of Campenhausen, Peter is the *"Stammvater,"* the patriarch from whom all church order derives.[38] We see here the first formulation of the patristic notion to appear later in a more developed form in the thought of Cyprian and Augustine. For them Peter is "the first bishop" possessing in himself the fullness of episcopacy from whom all other apostle-bishops derive their powers.[39]

Peter is presented not only as the foundation on which the whole church order is built but also as the active agent who builds up the church: "In him, that is, through him, was the church built up" (*Mod* 21.11).

Moreover, Peter also received the keys to the kingdom of heaven. This includes the "key of doctrine" (cf. Lk 11:52) by which he preached the words of salvation (*Mod* 21.11), the administration of baptism by which he provided entry into the heavenly kingdom (21.12), and the power to forgive sins (21.9).

Tertullian does not mention that Peter communicated his function of being the foundation of the church and of church order to any other person. But, according to Tertullian, Peter did hand over the power of the keys to the church:

> Remember that here (on earth) the Lord left the keys (of the kingdom of heaven) to Peter and through him to the church *(memento claves eius hic Dominum Petro et per eum Ecclesiae reliquisse)* (*Antidote* 10.8).

Thus every martyr of the church who confesses Jesus on earth carries the keys with him on his journey to heaven *(ibid.)*. Here again we find the beginning of an important doctrine to be expanded in later fathers: Peter received first what the Lord intended to give through him to the whole church. Note that attributing the power of keys to martyrs is not a Montanist innovation but part of Tertullian's Catholic background. In fact, the Catholic Tertullian ascribes more power to the martyrs than the Montanist. According to the latter, the martyr can obtain forgiveness only for himself (*Mod* 22.9–11), while the former agrees with the Catholic practice that the martyrs restored public sinners to the peace of the church. In *To Martyrs* he exhorts the martyrs to keep peace among themselves in prison because the public sinners

> used to ask from the martyrs in prison that peace which they did not have in the church. Therefore you ought to keep, nurture, and preserve that peace among yourselves for this reason so that, if needed, you may grant it to others (1.6).[40]

We know that this practice was not restricted to the church of Carthage. The letter of the martyrs of Vienne and Lyons, *pace* Poschmann, seems to imply the same practice[41] and so does a letter of Dionysius, bishop of Alexandria in the third century.[42] The Catholic Tertullian, however, is aware, as bishop Dionysius is, that the final arbiter and minister of public penance is the bishop of the local church.

If Peter received the power of keys for the whole church, we should now investigate how, according to Tertullian, this power was transmitted from Peter to the local church and her bishop.

"The Church Related to Peter's Church (Ecclesia Petri propinqua)"

What interests us primarily is the view of the Catholic Tertullian and the faith of the Catholic church in Carthage as reflected in the polemics of the Montanist Tertullian. Tertullian in his Catholic period does not exclude any grave sin from the church's power of reconciliation. Should a Christian sin gravely after baptism, he can be absolved if he confesses his sin and does public penance. The ecclesiastical character of penance is emphasized throughout *Penitence*. The penitent asks for the prayers of his brothers, prostrates himself at the feet of the presbyters and kneels before the altars of God. The result is, "While prostrating man, it (penance) raises him up, while making him dirty, it cleanses him, while accusing, it actually excuses him, while condemning, it actually absolves him" (8.4–6).

The Montanist Tertullian also admits that the church, which is "properly speaking and primarily the Spirit himself *(ipsa ecclesia proprie et principaliter ipse est spiritus),* has the power of forgiving sins" *(Mod* 21.16–17). However, only a spiritual person can exercise this power which he receives as a personal nontransmittable privilege. Such spiritually perfect individuals were the prophets and the apostles in the past, and the new prophets of Montanism in the present. Through the Montanist prophets the Paraclete announces: "The church has the power to forgive (the) sin (of adultery), but I will not do it lest they commit other sins, too" *(Mod* 21.7). The Montanist Tertullian rejects the Catholic view that the bishops can forgive grave sins. But, in the process of arguing against it, Tertullian formulates rather clearly the position of his Catholic adversary. His opponent is probably Agrippinus, the bishop of Carthage whom he mocks as *pontifex maximus* and *episcopus episcoporum.*[43]

> I now inquire into your position: on what basis do you usurp this right of the church (that of forgiving sins)? Just because the Lord said to Peter: "on this rock I will build my church; I will give you the keys of the heavenly kingdom," or "whatever you bind or loose on earth will be bound or loosed in heaven," you presume that the power of loosing and binding has reached down also to you, that is, to every church related to the church of Peter *(idcirco praesumis et ad te derivasse solvendi et alligandi potestatem, id est ad omnem ecclesiam Petri propinquam)?* What sort of man are you, that you turn upside down and change the manifest intention of the

Lord who conferred this (power) on the person of Peter?
He said, "Upon you will I build my church," and "what-
ever you loose or bind" not whatever they loose or bind
(*Mod* 21.9–10).

The key sentence is the one I quoted in Latin.[44] Two implications need to be clarified. The first is the subject of the power
of loosing and binding. The phrase *ad omnem ecclesiam Petri
propinquam* serves as an apposite to *ad te* and further explains
it. Thus, as Tertullian understands the Catholic view, the subject
of power is the bishop of the local church insofar as the bishop
embodies in himself the local church.

The second implication concerns the relationship of this
power to Peter. The local church and her bishop possess this
power only insofar as the local church is related *(propinqua)* to
that of Peter. In order to determine the nature of this relatedness,
we should compare this sentence to its close parallel in *Antidote*
10.8:

Remember that here (on earth) the Lord left the keys (of
the kingdom of heaven) to Peter and through him to the
church.
. . . you presume that the power of loosing and binding
has reached also to you, that is, to every church related
to Peter *(ad omnem ecclesiam Petri propinquam)?*

According to the first text, the Lord handed over the keys to
Peter and through him to the universal church. According to this
second one, the power possessed by the church of Peter, that is,
the church of Rome, has reached down "to all the churches
related to the church of Peter." If this parallelism is correct, "all
the churches related to that of Peter" must mean the universal
church. The term *propinqua,* then, does not simply refer to geo-
graphical proximity, political ties or relationship of foundation,
but to a relationship of origin in a theological sense which transcends historical origin. The text reflects the conviction of the
African church that the power of forgiving sins reaches down to
all the churches from the church of Peter. This interpretation is

confirmed by another text quoted earlier: Tertullian sees in Peter
the foundation for all church order, not only for those churches
which are in historical line of succession from him.[45]

CONCLUSION

The joint authority and the agreement of Peter and Paul in
all matters of doctrine is a central criterion in the theology of
both Irenaeus and Tertullian. For both, in some sense, Peter and
Paul represent all the apostles. Besides these two, only John and
James are mentioned with any frequency. In Irenaeus, even
though Peter is almost always mentioned first when he appears
together with Paul, both apostles seem to have equal authority.
In Tertullian we noticed a tendency to subordinate Paul to Peter
and to the "other pillars." Both theologians use the agreement
between Peter and Paul to prove those doctrines which are
denied by Marcion and the gnostics. Regarding the origin of their
agreement, Irenaeus points to the common revelation both Peter
and Paul received directly from the same God and Jesus his Son,
while Tertullian stresses the "handshake" between Peter and
Paul in Jerusalem as recorded in Galatians 2.

For the first time in patristic literature, Tertullian quotes,
repeatedly, Matthew 16:18–19. There is no indication that Tertullian himself was the first to note the importance of this passage; he often refers to it casually by way of an abbreviated quotation or allusion, as to a common heritage well-known by his
audience in the church of Africa. Through the interpretation of
that text the figure of Peter emerges in relation to Christ as the
rock upon which that church is founded.

Tertullian's christological interpretation of Matthew 16:18–
19 shows how misguided was the effort of post-tridentine Catholic exegesis which tried to prove that in Matthew 16:18-19 and
in its patristic exegesis, Peter himself and not the person of Jesus
is meant to be the rock of the church.[46] For Tertullian, just as
later for Origen, Augustine, and many other fathers, such opposition does not make sense. For them the two assertions, "Jesus
is the rock of the church" and "Peter himself is the rock" are both
in some sense true and need to be stated in connection with each

other, as two aspects of the same mystery.[47] The key for such a synthesis is an understanding of Matthew 16:18–19 in the light of Pauline ecclesiology according to which Jesus alone is the rock and foundation of the Church (1 Cor 10:4; 3:11). This harmonization presupposes a doctrine of participation which Tertullian used, as it were, instinctively. He was led to do so from the impact of the paradoxical nature of the Christian mystery rather than as a result of philosophical speculation.

With regard to the normativity of the church of Rome, two lines of interpretation emerged. Irenaeus based the *potentior principalitas* of Rome on its joint foundation by the two apostles Peter and Paul and on their martyrdom as a constitutive part of that foundation. The early Tertullian further developed this interpretation by adding to the martyrdom of the apostles Peter and Paul in Rome the quasi-martyrdom of the apostle John so that the word of God might stand on the testimony of three witnesses.

The Montanist Tertullian, however, in his polemics against African Catholics, attests to another way by which Catholics explain the authority of the church of Rome. Relying on an interpretation of Matthew 16:18–19 (possibly seen in conjunction with Matthew 18:18), the African church is convinced that the Lord first gave the power of the keys to Peter and through Peter to all the churches in communion with the church of Peter. Thus, according to this second line of thought, the normative position of Rome is based on the fact that it is the church of Peter. Here again we witness in Tertullian the first "sketch" of an important insight to be developed later by the fathers, in particular by Cyprian and Augustine but also in the eastern churches: Peter is the first apostle or bishop in the sense that he first received the fullness of apostolic powers from Christ to be handed on through him to all the bishops of the church. Yet, as the next chapter will show, the original grounding of the importance of the church of Rome upon the joint role of the two martyr apostles Peter and Paul will not be forgotten in the subsequent development of the church's tradition.

Chapter Four

HISTORICAL SURVEY
AND SYSTEMATIC REFLECTIONS

After investigating the joint role of Peter and Paul regarding the church of Rome in the thought of the two most important theologians of the second century, I will here summarize in two theses those "primitive" traditions which I found in Irenaeus and Tertullian and whose survival and further development I intend to sketch out in this chapter. While eclipsed from time to time by the theme of Petrine primacy, these first and second century traditions will be shown to have continued in the Roman Catholic church up to our day. Then, from the results of this survey, some conclusions will be drawn for Catholic systematic theology. The two theses are as follows:

I.   The church of Rome has been jointly founded by Peter and Paul. Consequently, the bishop of Rome acts by the authority of both Peter and Paul.

II.   According to the New Testament and the early patristic view, the martyrdom of the two chief apostles is constitutive of their apostolic mission, and their martyrdom in the city of Rome is constitutive of the leadership role of the church of Rome.

I will now examine these one at a time.

Thesis I

The church of Rome has been jointly founded by Peter and Paul.[1] Consequently, the bishop of Rome acts by the authority of both Peter and Paul.

Testimony to the Joint Foundation and the
Joint Role of Peter and Paul in Rome

The joint importance of Peter and Paul, including an insistence on their equality from a certain perspective, has survived the centuries. I shall mention here only a few testimonies. The Synod of Arles (314 A.D.) in a letter to Pope Sylvester attributes the prominence of the Roman church to the fact that "the apostles (Peter and Paul) sit (in judgment) every day (in Rome) and their blood bears witness unceasingly to the glory of God."[2]

St. Leo the Great, who sees in the bishop of Rome the successor of Peter, emphasizes nevertheless that both Peter and Paul are "the fathers" of the city. By inserting it into the heavenly kingdom, they founded the city in a much more excellent manner than those who laid the first foundations of its walls, one of whom also stained the city by fratricide. Clearly, Leo compares Peter and Paul to Romulus and Remus, the traditional founders of Rome. The first Rome was the "teacher of error," the second, through Peter and Paul, became "the disciple of the truth."[3] Moreover, the grace of God has set Peter and Paul so high as to be the "twin light of the eyes in the body whose head is Christ."[4]

The author of the *Decretum Gelasianum,* who like Leo stresses that Rome is "the first see of the apostle Peter" and received its primacy among the other patriarchal sees through the words of the Lord addressed to Peter (Mt 16:18–19), still adds another reason for its special dignity.

To whom (Peter) has been added the company of Paul, the vessel of election, who, not as the heretics jabber at a different time, but at one and the same time, on the same day, fighting under Nero, was crowned along with Peter with a glorious death in the city of Rome. They equally consecrated the above-mentioned holy Roman church to Christ the Lord, and by their presence and venerable triumph they made it more distinguished among all the cities of the entire world.[5]

Beginning with Nicholas I (858–867) there is a new emphasis on the fact that the bishop of Rome is endowed with the joint authority of Peter and Paul.[6] According to Nicholas' letter to Emperor Michael III of Byzantium, the pope received his special position by God's decree "through blessed Peter and in blessed Paul." The pope enjoys his rights "through the supreme power of the blessed apostles Peter and Paul." Nicholas refers to himself as born and constituted by divine grace a son to these fathers even though he is unworthy and unequal in merit with them.[7] From this time on the Roman see always introduced its solemn acts, such as convocation of councils, doctrinal definitions, canonizations and bestowal of spiritual favors, by the formula "auctoritate Apostolorum Petri et Pauli."[8] Pius IX used the phrase in the bull which defines the immaculate conception, as did Pius XII in the one which defines the assumption.[9]

As far as back as it can be attested (258 A.D.), the liturgy has always celebrated the memory of Peter and Paul jointly both in the west and the east. It is important to note that the new *Missale Romanum* promulgated by Pope Paul VI in 1970 has abolished the separate celebration of Paul on June 30 and renewed the ancient tradition of their common feast on June 29. Paul VI renewed the memory of the joint foundation of Rome by Peter and Paul in the consciousness of the church by stressing its importance for the church of Rome on numerous occasions. When he points to the apostolic source of the Catholic faith in the church of Rome, he mentions in a particular way Peter and Paul.

> Within the . . . group (of the apostles) [Christ] gave a special place to Peter as shepherd of shepherds and to Paul an extraordinary authority, for, as the latter says of himself: "I have been made its (the truth's) herald and apostle . . . the teacher of the nations in the true faith" (1 Tim 2:7).[10]

The reaffirmation of this ancient tradition by the magisterium calls attention to its enduring value. We cannot say that attributing the theological importance of the church of Rome to its being founded by the two martyr apostles Peter and Paul is merely a less perfect, provisional formulation of a later, more adequate doctrine, namely that the bishop of Rome is the vicar (or in a nuanced sense the successor) of Peter. In other words, the theological importance of the church of Rome is not based only upon the fact that its bishop is the vicar of Peter; the earlier ground for the primacy is not simply more primitive and less valid than the latter. The theological content of the first has not been adequately explicated by the second. As in many cases of doctrinal development, a necessary refinement and articulation has been achieved at the expense of neglecting other aspects of a more encompassing truth of faith.

The Implications of the Joint Role of Peter and Paul for the Church of Rome

Our task, then, is to attempt to uncover the other aspects of this "more encompassing truth" implicit in the historically original grounding of Rome's primacy.

1.   The Petrine Heritage

First we need to summarize the connection between Peter and the papacy. The church gradually came to understand, and then define at Vatican I, that Peter has received from Christ the mission to be the supreme visible center of unity for the church in matters of both doctrine and praxis.[11] This center must exist as long as the church does, until the end of human history. However, if we search for the actual existence of this center in the church we find historical evidence only for the church of Rome which early tradition considers to have been founded by Peter and Paul. Moreover, the bishops of Rome, beginning at least with Pope Victor at the end of the second century, have de facto shown the awareness of having the power to exclude local churches from the communion of the universal Catholic church. This is the historical basis on which the Catholic dogma of Petrine succession rests: as bishop of Rome, the pope succeeds to Peter in the sense that Peter continues through the pope his ministry for the unity of the church.

However, beyond this formal connection of being a successor of Peter, the bishop of Rome, in a broader but more comprehensive sense, may be called to be an heir to Peter. Succession implies that the succeeding person continues the office of his predecessor. The heir does not have to continue the same office but he receives a heritage to protect, guard and increase. Peter's heritage is his confession of faith in the earthly Jesus embodied in all the four gospels and his witness (the first of all the apostles) to the risen Christ. In a more general sense, his apostolic authority confirms both the traditions of the synoptic gospels and that of John. Through his confession of faith he is also the foundation on which Jesus has built his church. The bishop of Rome, then, as an heir to Peter, is called to preserve and actualize in every age this Petrine heritage.

2.   The Pauline Heritage

What is the relationship of the church of Rome and of the bishop of Rome to Paul? The popes occasionally called themselves successors of Peter and Paul.[12] Insofar as Paul is an apostle, and every bishop in the college of bishops succeeds to all apostles, the pope as bishop succeeds to Paul in a similar sense as he succeeds to all the apostles.

Paul, however, has a very special position among the apostles.

(a)   He is the "thirteenth apostle" "born out of due time" whose addition to the original "twelve" was not foreseen by the beginning church. His call bears witness to the sovereign power of the risen Christ over the institution. He seeks communion with the existing pillars of the church but attributes his authority directly to the risen Christ.[13]

(b)   Paul is also unique in the sense that, by understanding the universality of Christ's redemption through the pure grace of God, he presents the first coherent theology. Thus, in the words of the tradition and liturgy, he has become the *doctor,* the teacher. While Peter's function is the *principatus,* the primacy, Paul's is the *doctrina,* the theological teaching.

(c)   Moreover, Paul does more than any other apostle to open up the church to the world of the Gentiles. He shows how the gospel transcends all cultures and embraces the whole world. He has thus become "the apostle to the Gentiles."

(d)   The Pauline writings (attributable to him according to various degrees of authorship) dominate the second half of the

New Testament canon, but his theology influences also its first half—at least three, and perhaps all, of the gospels.

This special vocation of Paul discussed above is such a unique personal charism that no one can, in the strict sense, succeed him. Part of Paul's vocation is to show forth the absolute freedom of God's grace which shakes up and pushes the institution to transcend its own limits. Institutionalizing the Pauline vocation to a Pauline "office" into which one juridically succeeds would be to tame the Pauline heritage to the point of eliminating it.

Thus, instead of a Pauline succession, it would be more precise to speak about a Pauline heritage to which the bishop of Rome is to remain committed. We may then say that the bishop of the church of Rome is called to be an heir no less to Paul than to Peter.[14] Just as the bishop of Rome cannot claim to fulfill Peter's role as the chief witness to the earthly life of Jesus and as the first witness to Jesus' resurrection, in a similar way no pope can claim for himself the unique gifts of Paul, but every pope is called to preserve, promote, and interpret Paul's heritage and remain open to the unpredictable charismatic "Pauline" gift of the spirit.

3. The Joint Heritage

The bishop of Rome's vocation of fostering the twofold heritage of Peter and Paul can be further expanded in the following ways.

(a)   Just as in the early times the church of Rome continued the Jerusalem agreement of Peter and Paul (and James and John) by integrating into its canon the writings produced under the authority of these men, the mission of the bishop of Rome is to continue to preach and interpret the united witness of the whole New Testament.

(b)   As Peter is the chief witness to the earthly life and passion of Jesus, so Paul is to the power of the risen Lord who rules his church in the Spirit.[15] The Roman bishop's being an heir to both means that he bears witness to the identity of Jesus of Nazareth with the risen Lord, to the identity of the institutional church (which goes back to the twelve appointed by the earthly Jesus) with the church of the Spirit.[16]

(c)   As an heir to Paul, the bishop of Rome will be open to all the charisms of the Spirit, testing all manifestations and encouraging the authentic charisms, but, like both Peter and Paul, subordinating them to apostolic authority.[17]

(d)   In carrying out the ministry of Peter, he is the guardian against distortions and the harmonizer of the various trends of the Christian tradition. In fidelity to the mission of Paul, he is the missionary to the Gentiles.[18] Just as Paul always made sure that he remained in collegial agreement with the other apostles, so the pope will seek and promote collegial consensus but not refrain from taking personal initiative to disengage the church from a too exclusive identification with one nation, continent or culture. He will open her up to speak to new cultures and "incarnate" her very same life and doctrine in new forms of new cultures.

If we investigate the history of the church in the light of the above "job description" for the pope as an heir to both Peter and Paul, we cannot help observing that many bishops of Rome were actually aware of this twofold vocation. They traditionally expressed their role of being a "vicar of Peter" in Pauline terms. For instance, in the patristic age it became a tradition for the pope to designate his office by a typical Pauline phrase, *sollicitudo omnium ecclesiarum,* "concern for all the churches" (2 Cor 11:28). From the beginning to the present there is much evidence that the popes considered themselves as the missionary to the nations. In fact, many of the major missionary thrusts of the western church (to England, to some of the Slavic nations, to Hungary, to Latin America, Africa and Asia) were initiated by Rome.

While Rome consistently rejected charismatic movements which put the personal authority of the charismatic above the bearer of apostolic authority,[19] the best popes allied themselves with what they discovered as genuine manifestations of the Spirit. For instance, they used the spiritual energies of the Benedictine, Cistercian and Franciscan reform movements to renew the institutional church. Thus it was in the line of the best Petrine-Pauline tradition for John XXIII to liberate the forces of renewal by calling together Vatican II. It is no accident that Roger Schütz, the Protestant prior of Taizé, and Mother Teresa, two of the greatest charismatics of our time, are presently so closely associated with the church of Rome.

As his chosen name attests, among recent popes Paul VI was most aware that his vocation must reflect that of both Peter and Paul. A few months before his death, in his last homily on the feast of Peter and Paul he summarized the fifteen years of his pontificate in the words of Peter and Paul.

Looking at them (Peter and Paul) we review briefly the period of time during which the Lord entrusted his church to us; and even though we consider ourselves the last and unworthy successor of Peter, we feel comforted and uplifted at this last threshold (of our life) by the awareness that we kept repeating tirelessly before the church and the world, "You are the Christ, the Son of the living God," and, just as Paul, we too may say, "I have fought the good fight, finished my course and kept the faith."[20]

THESIS II

The martyrdom of the two chief apostles is constitutive of their apostolic mission, and their martyrdom in the city of Rome is constitutive of the leadership role of the church of Rome.

Martyrdom and Apostolic Mission

In the early church the fact that the chief apostles became martyrs was not seen as something merely extrinsic and accidental to their apostolic mission. Nor was it understood as merely a human confirmation of the witness' veracity. Certainly, the martyr testifies that his human life is less precious than the gospel for whose sake he surrenders his life and thereby points with his own human existence to its truth. But what really matters in the act of martyrdom for the early church is that Christ himself testifies in and through the human martyr. Christ himself suffers and triumphs over death in the martyr and thus the martyr reveals the power and glory of Christ in his suffering. He becomes so transparent that his testimony is no longer just a human voice but he himself can be called "logos theou," the true and powerful word of God himself.[21] This explains why martyrdom is essential to the apostolic ministry. It perfects the apostle in his function as apostle.

There is a close connection between what happens to Jesus and what happened to the martyr apostles in their death. Jesus entered his reign and rules his church in the form of the Lamb who has been slain and is alive forever. The apostles who shared in the suffering of Christ also share in his reign: they sit with him in judgment, but they sit in their act of being martyred, for their "blood attests God's glory unceasingly."[22]

Their "judging" does not begin at the last judgment. As the expectation of an early parousia faded away, the apostolic church, upon a canonical reading of the New Testament, has gradually come to understand how the promise of Jesus about the coming of the kingdom is being fulfilled. Through his death and resurrection Christ has become king. He reigns as the only *kyrios* over the universe and, in a particular way, he reigns in his church. Even though the final coming of the kingdom is still in the future, those who serve him faithfully, especially the martyrs, join Christ in his reign upon their death. In particular, the apostles begin to sit in judgment over the church from the time of their martyrdom up to the end of the ages. Thus the kingdom is both a future and present reality, or, more precisely, the eschatological future (which is the glorified Christ with his saints, especially with the apostles and martyrs and, even more prominently, with the martyr-apostles) is present and active in the church.[23] The kingdom penetrates the church in an invisible but effective way and assures the march of the church toward the final realization of the kingdom. The apostles, then, exercise their function of "judging" in the church throughout her history.

The liturgy of the church has always kept this truth alive and explains in more detail what this activity of "judging" entails. For instance, the preface of the apostles in the Roman liturgy addresses God the Father in this way:

You, eternal shepherd, never abandon your flock, but continue to guard them through your blessed apostles,

> so that they may be guided by the same rulers whom
> you have appointed as substitute shepherds *(vicarios . . .*
> *pastores)* over them in order to carry out your work.[24]

The text makes clear that God the Father is the eternal shepherd
of the flock who does not cease to be the shepherd when he
chooses the apostles. Rather, he carries out his work through the
blessed apostles who are only substitute or deputy shepherds representing the Father. Nor does the shepherding of the apostles
cease with their death. Their apostolic ministry lasts throughout
the whole history of the church. God wants the very same rulers
to govern his church up to the very end of history. So there is no
succession here but rather representation and participation. The
eternal shepherding of the Father becomes manifest and effective
through the shepherding of the apostles. The present work of the
apostles is so much emphasized that the work of the bishops,
who, according to the faith of the church, continue the apostolic
ministry, is not even mentioned.

The liturgy does not take the governing and shepherding
activity of the apostles in the juridical sense to which we are
accustomed. From the viewpoint of the liturgy, their governing
takes the form of intercessory prayer with God. As one ancient
prayer puts it concisely, "The church is governed by their
prayers."[25]

If the apostles do not stop functioning in the church then we
must speak of "representation" and "participation" as well as of
"apostolic succession." The college of bishops did not simply
succeed to that of the apostles, as one governing body of an institution is replaced by its legitimate successors. The apostles are
not replaced, they remain present and carry out their work
through the college of bishops up to the end of the world. Whenever the college of bishops acts together (including their head, the
bishop of Rome) and whenever an individual bishop or a group
of bishops acts as part of that college (that is, in union with each
other and with their head), they make present the apostolic college and carry out its ministry.

Not only does the college of the bishops succeed to the college of the apostles; the latter are present and active in the former.
This distinguishes the Catholic doctrine of apostolic succession

from a merely juridical model applicable to many institutions besides the Catholic church.[26] What makes this unique "being in one another" possible is the Holy Spirit. As the transcendent principle of unity in the church, he enables the apostles to carry out their ministry through the ministry of the bishops of every generation. Because of the Holy Spirit, the apostles and the bishops of every age—in fact, the church of the apostles and the church of every subsequent age—constitute more than just one moral person, a merely juridical entity; in some sense, the two are one and the same reality.

What we have said up to now applies to the relationship between all the apostles and all the bishops of the church and also to the relationship between all the apostles and all the local churches. What, then, is special to the relationship between Peter and Paul and the bishop of Rome, between Peter and Paul and the church of Rome?

Presence of the Martyr Apostles Peter and Paul in Rome

The liturgy celebrated at the shrines which were built at the tombs of martyrs and saints expresses the faith of the church that by entering the transcendent realm of God through death the apostle, the martyr or the saint acquires a special presence at his or her grave and in the community where he or she lived. This intimate presence of the martyr (and later of the saint) at the grave and in the worshiping community, as a result of his intimate presence with God, is a uniquely Christian phenomenon which cannot be deduced from previous pagan practices.[27] This is one concrete way in which the kingdom, consummated in Christ and in his saints, penetrates our world and becomes effective in it. According to the testimony of the church's liturgy, the intercessory influence of the saints is attested especially in that place and community in which their earthly bodily existence evolved and came to be consummated and where their bodies were buried.

This applies in a special way to the martyr apostles, Peter and Paul. Through his martyrdom Rome becomes the birthplace of Paul, according to Tertullian.[28] The graffiti on the walls of San

Sebastiano near the via Appia show that the cult of Peter and Paul was firmly established there in the first half of the third century.[29] People have prayed for their intercession. Numerous prayers in the liturgy express the awareness that the church of Rome is taught, governed and ruled by these two apostles throughout the ages. When the church of Rome was in mortal danger, the popes frequently called upon the intercession of Peter and Paul to save that church.[30] When Cyril of Alexandria reached an agreement with John of Antioch on a common confession of faith in Christ, Pope Xystus explained in his letter to Cyril how appropriate it was to celebrate the reunion of the churches at a synod in St. Peter's Basilica in Rome. In this way Peter himself presided over the triumphant celebration, the same Peter who took part in the struggle to restore the unity of faith.[31] In other texts, for instance in one by Cardinal Deusdedit in the eleventh century, both Peter and Paul are said to "live and preside in the church of Rome."[32]

The intercessory prayer of Peter and Paul is invoked not only in Rome and in the western churches which received their liturgy from Rome. The Byzantine church also prays to Christ:

> Through their prayers (of blessed Peter and Paul), overcome our invisible enemies, O Christ God, and make firm our Orthodox faith, for you are the Lover of Mankind.[33]

At least from the fourth century onward the presence of Peter in the church of Rome not only is affirmed in a general way but is connected especially with the person of the bishop of Rome. The popes begin to refer to their own service as the one through which the blessed Peter carries out his ministry for all the churches. For instance, thus writes Pope Siricius:

> We carry the burden of all who are burdened; in fact, the blessed apostle Peter carries these burdens in us, he who, as we trust, protects and defends us in everything as the heirs to his office.[34]

Typically, Pope Xystus describes the activity of Peter in his successors in Pauline terms:

> The blessed apostle Peter has handed on in his successors what he has received.[35]

What Paul says about his activity in Corinth in 1 Corinthians 15:3, the Roman bishop transfers to the transhistorical activity of Peter throughout the centuries.

Not only do the popes assert this active presence of Peter in themselves, but the church also professes this belief. For instance, as we have seen above, at the Council of Ephesus, Peter is said to live and judge in his successors.[36] Yet at the same council the pope is also hailed as a new Paul because of his right judgment on the doctrine of Nestorius.[37]

The above texts are only illustrations of the generally attested belief throughout the centuries that Peter and Paul are present in a special way in the church of Rome. They intercede for it and thereby rule and protect it. Moreover, Peter, described by features borrowed from Paul, carries out his ministry in a special way through the bishop of Rome.

One more dimension of the relationship between the apostles and the pope needs some explanation: How does the pope's teaching activity relate to that of Peter and Paul? As Pope Xystus' letter which I quoted above attests, in his official capacity the pope does not simply "continue" the teaching of Peter and Paul and of the other apostles; he actualizes in every new age the same apostolic teaching and in particular that tradition which Peter has received. In fact, the pope's act of teaching is in some real sense Peter's act. Peter is the subject to whom the teachings of succeeding popes must be attributed. It is Peter who "hands on in his successors what he has received." However, while it is always Peter who is said to carry out his ministry through the pope, this "Peter" includes also the features and the doctrine of Paul. Moreover, as we have seen, in his most solemn acts the pope acts with the joint authority of both Peter and Paul.

It is also important to notice that the teaching activity of the pope is often described as judging, and he teaches from his *kathedra* or *thronos* or *sedes.* A more thorough investigation would probably show that these terms and some of the texts speaking about the judging activity of the bishop of Rome have originally had some reference to the eschatological texts of the Bible such as Matthew 19:28.[38] His teaching is an eschatological act of judging through which the apostles Peter and Paul exercise the judge's role promised to them by Christ in Matthew 19:28. This means that, by discerning the pure gospel of Christ and by rejecting errors, Peter and Paul assure that the apostolic see remains immaculate and stainless, ready for the bridegroom's return.[39]

Pope Paul VI, who looked to these two apostles as models and inspirers during his pontificate, at the end of his life asked for their prayers to protect the church.

Saints Peter and Paul, you brought into the world the name of Christ and gave him the ultimate witness of love and blood; protect now and always this Church for which you have lived and died. Guard it in the truth and in peace. Increase in all her sons an unshakeable fidelity to the Word of God. . . .[40]

CONCLUSIONS

The meaning of the tradition concerning the martyrdom and the continued presence and activity of Peter and Paul in Rome may be summarized in the following way.

1. If we accept the faith of the church of the fathers on how the kingdom came to be realized, the opposition disappears between the promise of Jesus about the imminent arrival of the kingdom and what really happened after his crucifixion (an opposition so uncritically cultivated ever since the nineteenth century German Protestant quest for the historical Jesus). Through his death and crucifixion Jesus does indeed enter upon his reign, and the martyr apostles (along with the other martyrs and all the saints who in some way participate through their own bodies in the death and resurrection of Christ) join him in his reign. The kingdom thus consummated in Jesus and the saints penetrates

the church and is active in the church throughout her history. Yet the church is not to be identified with the kingdom whose manifest coming is expected at the end of time.[41]

2. The shepherding and teaching of the bishops must be seen within this context of the invisible but real presence of the kingdom in the church. When the bishops fulfill their ministry according to God's will, the college of the apostles carries out their ministry through them. Thus whatever good the bishops of a certain age accomplish has some special causal connection with the concern, love and prayer of the apostles (not denying, of course, the intercession of all the saints). The visible activity of the hierarchy is only "the tip of the iceberg." The church on earth never acts separately from the church in heaven, and the episcopal ministry, insofar as it is supernaturally fruitful, is only the visible side of the apostolic ministry in heaven.

3. The shepherding and teaching of the bishop of Rome must also be seen in this context. His function of primacy and his share in the infallibility of the church are based on the fact that he is a successor of Peter. These facts are hereby not denied. Yet, if we look at the pope's work in the context of the kingdom inchoatively present in the church or, in other words, in the context of the *communio sanctorum,* the living influence in the church of Rome of both Peter and Paul must be affirmed. Whatever good the pope's ministry accomplishes for the church of Rome and for the universal church is (beyond the cooperation of all the saints and particularly the apostles) causally linked to the concern, love and prayer of both martyr apostles Peter and Paul who "live and preside in the church of Rome."

In this perspective the juridical structures of the church are neither abolished nor given more efficacy than is required by dogmatic teaching. This view still allows for imprudent or harmful acts on the part of the pope and even for infallible and yet inopportune dogmatic definitions. It only says that whatever in the pope's activity truly builds up the church is connected with the governing activity (through intercessory prayer) of the two chief apostles.

4. In this context, we perceive that the church of today is not only in continuity with the church of the apostles but is, in

some real sense, identical with it. This identity is both a fact but also a task to be constantly renewed and reactualized. Herein lies also its ecumenical significance. The Roman Catholic church must again, and again, reroot its present teaching in that of the apostles and recheck any doctrinal development against the permanent norm of apostolic teaching as it has been put into writing in the books of the New Testament. This does not imply the acceptance of the fundamentalist position according to which non-biblical terminology cannot express a binding truth of faith. Nor does it accept the historical critic's contention that every church teaching is valid only if the historical critical method can prove its derivation from biblical teaching. It rather means that the overall balance of church teachings and of theological synthesis should reflect the balance of scriptures. In other words, what is central in biblical teaching ought to be central also in the proclamation and in the theological systems of the present day church.

5.   The union of the earthly and heavenly church, the presence of the apostles in the bishops and the presence of Peter and Paul in the church of Rome is made possible by the transcendent principle of unity and interiority, the Holy Spirit. His transcendent activity maintains the unity of the church throughout the ages so that it becomes more than just a succession of one generation to another, accepting the same beliefs and rule of life. He assures the presence of the apostles in the church on earth throughout the ages. This "active ministry of the apostles" as well as the cooperation of all the saints in the work of the church on earth does not diminish the power of God's grace but rather gives glory to God from whom all the glory and efficacy of his saints derive. The Byzantine liturgy expresses admirably this theological and doxological dimension of the cult of the apostles:

> Today Christ the Rock glorifies with supreme honor the Rock of Faith and Leader of the Apostles, together with Paul and the Company of the Twelve, whose memory we celebrate with eagerness of faith, giving glory to the One who gave glory to them.[42]

Chapter Five

A RESPONSE TO CHAPTER 4
FROM A PROTESTANT
PERSPECTIVE

Since the purpose of Chapter 4 has been for Kereszty to draw out some conclusions for Roman Catholic systematic theology from the results of his survey of the "primitive" tradition which he found in Irenaeus and Tertullian, and in the survival and further development of that tradition, it is only fitting that by way of response I set down in writing both what (from a Protestant perspective) I perceive as promising and what I perceive as problem-causing in these conclusions. In the spirit of the purpose of the book as a whole, this will be done with an eye to explicating further convergence in our thinking about these matters, as well as to noting which conclusions of Kereszty, or which parts of some of his conclusions, would appear to be unacceptable to or, as stated, problem-causing for Protestants (perhaps I should say for Protestants who share my perception of the nature of the holy catholic church). This brings us to an important point, namely, in what sense we are using the terms Catholic and Protestant in this discussion.

When Kereszty writes (p. 82) that he will draw some conclusions for "Catholic systematic theology," I take it everyone understands that he means "Catholic" from his perspective, which is a *"Roman* Catholic" perspective. And it is clear from the way in which I have expressed myself that I realize that as a Protestant I can hardly represent Protestants in general, but at best I may hope that in some measure I may represent those who share my perception of the nature of the holy catholic church.

I have been nurtured in a tradition where I have been taught to confess my belief in the holy catholic church according to an ancient creed going back to the period of Irenaeus and Tertullian. While I may not have understood fully what it meant or means to confess this "apostolic" faith, specifically, my belief in the "holy catholic church," I have nonetheless for as long as I can remember repeated this part of the Apostles' Creed with a clear conscience. Exactly how the Roman Catholic church was or is related to the holy catholic church has never been clear to me. This effort to understand the role of the apostles Peter and Paul in founding the church of Rome is my first attempt to reflect systematically on the larger question of the relationship of the holy catholic church, in which I profess belief, to that Roman Catholic church which I am coming to know and beginning to understand through the several avenues of communication that have been opened up by Vatican Council II for genuine conversation and academic colleagueship between Protestants and Roman Catholics.

"Founding" by Martyrdom

In the opening paragraph of Chapter 4 (p. 82), Kereszty, in formulating his first thesis, encounters an important problem of definition with which it is fitting for us to begin our response. His first thesis reads, "The church of Rome has been jointly founded by Peter and Paul." In a footnote Kereszty goes on to say, "In the light of today's historical evidence this joint 'founding' must be interpreted as a theological assertion with some historical foundation rather than a strictly historical statement describing a merely historical process." Kereszty explains (p. 146, n. 1):

> The Christian community in Rome did already exist before Paul, and probably, before Peter came to that city. They "founded" the church of Rome by making it the depository of their apostolic teaching and by confirming their teaching with their martyrdom. In the words of Tertullian, the apostles "poured their whole

teaching along with their blood" into the church of Rome (*Pre* 36.3).

It is a matter of great importance for the ongoing discussion to clarify and respond to the distinction that Fr. Roch is making. Apart from the joint martyrdom of the apostles Peter and Paul in Rome there is no reason to distinguish the Christian community in that city from the Christian community in any other city. Rome was the capital city of the empire. As the capital city to which "all roads led," it was natural if not inevitable that Christians, following these roads from different parts of the empire, would meet in Rome. This simple fact would not in and of itself lead to the foundation of an organized church in Rome. No doubt relatively soon there were various house churches existing in different parts of the city where Christians could meet and celebrate their faith. So far as history can tell us anything about the actual origin of the Christian community in Rome, Paul's letter to the Romans provides us the earliest information we have. He addresses his letter "To all God's beloved in Rome, who are called to be saints" (1:7a). He mentions the fact that their faith "is proclaimed in all the world" (1:8b). Paul has "often intended to come" to them (1:13). He exhorts them: "May the God of steadfastness and encouragement grant you to live in such harmony with one another in accord with Christ Jesus, that together you may with one voice glorify the God and Father of our Lord Jesus Christ" (15:5–6). He mentions the many times he has "been hindered in coming" to them (15:22). And he specifically refers to the "many years" that he has longed to come to them and writes, "I hope to see you in passing as I go to Spain, and to be sped on my journey there by you, once I have enjoyed your company for a little" (15:23–24). In concluding his letter he reiterates his plan to go by Rome on his way to Spain and writes "I know that when I come to you I shall come in the fullness of the blessing of Christ" (15:28b–29). His final words are as follows: "I appeal to you, brethren, by our Lord Jesus Christ and by the love of the Spirit, to strive together with me in your prayers to God on my behalf, that I may be delivered from the unbelievers in Judea, and that my service for Jerusalem may be acceptable to the saints, so that by God's will I may come to you with joy and be refreshed in your company. The God of peace be with you all. Amen" (15:30–33).

From all of this it is clear that there had been a Christian community in Rome for many years at the time Paul wrote this letter. It must have had the reputation of being a community that had the resources to supply missionaries and speed them on their way. But whether it was a community that was organized to do this is not clear. Paul appears to be at pains to exhort them to act in "harmony with one another" (15:5), and to "strive together" with him in prayers to God on his behalf to the end that he might come to them with joy and "be refreshed" in their company (15:32).

By way of comparison to the manner in which Paul addresses Christians in his other letters, there is nothing in what he says to "God's beloved in Rome" that indicates that their church life is any more or any less structured or centralized or under episcopal care than was the church life in Christian communities in other cities to which Paul addressed letters. There is some supervisional care being expressed by Paul in his letter to God's beloved in Rome. It is a care being extended to Christians living in Rome that is authorized by the apostolic mandate, recognized and confirmed by the Jerusalem apostles, that had been given to Paul to evangelize the Gentiles (Rom 1:1–6).

Paul himself uses language which suggests that he thought of himself as founding some churches when he writes, "From Jerusalem and as far round as Illyricum I have fully preached the gospel of Christ, thus making it my ambition to preach the gospel, not where Christ has already been named, lest I build on another man's foundation." It is clear that he did not in this sense of the word "found" the church in Rome. Such evangelical foundations had already been laid in Rome long before Paul wrote his letter to the Romans, and they had not been laid by him, since until then he had never preached the gospel in Rome, nor for that matter in any place west of Illyricum.

It is one thing to preach the gospel. It is another to lay down one's life for the sake of the gospel. Certain foundations for the church can be laid in a given community through preaching. But no amount of preaching can produce the effect of martyrdom. A community which experiences martyrdom experiences a metaphysical shock of the deepest order with profound sociological repercussions. In order to understand the church of Rome, it seems to me, we must attempt to imagine the ontic shock within the Christian community of Rome that resulted from the martyrdom of not only that chief apostle to whom the apostles in Jerusalem had given the right hand of fellowship, that he should be entrusted with the mission to the Gentiles, but also that other chief apostle to whom the apostles in Jerusalem had entrusted the evangelization of the Jews. The two heads of these two apostolic missions had been brought low in the capital city of the Roman empire. What more devastating blow could have been struck against this fledgling movement within the life of the *oikoumenē?* And yet this most devastating blow seems only to have strengthened and deepened the faith, first of Christians in Rome, and then the faith of all Christians everywhere who stood in the martyrological tradition of Jesus and understood the martyrdom of the two chief apostles of the church as examples of being obedient unto death, in accordance with Jesus' apostolic commission:

> Behold, I send you out as sheep in the midst of wolves,
> so be wise as serpents and innocent as doves.
> Beware of men; for they will deliver you up to councils and
>   flay you in their synagogues,
> And you will be dragged before governors and kings for my
>   sake
> to bear testimony before them and the Gentiles.
> When they deliver you up,
> do not be anxious how you are to speak or what you are to
>   say;
> for what you are to say will be given to you in that hour;
> for it is not you who speak, but the Spirit of your Father
>   speaking through you.
> Brother will deliver up brother to death, and the father his
>   child,
> and children will rise against parents and have them put to
>   death;

and you will be hated by all for my name's sake.
But he who endures to the end will be saved (Mt 10:16–
23).

The martyrdom of Peter and Paul in Rome is not to be understood as the occasion for the emergence of a new cult for the founding of a new Roman civilization in which Peter and Paul are to replace Romulus and Remus, the legendary twin founders of Rome. However, it cannot be denied that it is instructive to view medieval and modern Rome from this perspective. Thus, for example, one can stand in the Piazza di San Pietro and see from a distance, lining the top of the façade of St. Peter's, Christ and his twelve apostles, while in the immediate foreground of the piazza itself one can sense being overshadowed by the heroic statues of Peter and Paul who dominate the scene as twin founders of a new Roman civilization—a civilization as glorious as anything ever produced out of the more ancient cult of Romulus and Remus. However instructive such a sociological and historical analysis of medieval and modern Rome may be, I am now persuaded that it represents a fundamental misreading of the monumental evidence. The church of Rome through the architecture of Saint Peter's and that of the Piazza di San Pietro is saying to the world, at the burial place of Peter, that Christ is at the center with his twelve disciple-apostles on either side of him—high and lifted up for all to see atop St. Peter's façade as the exalted rulers of the church—and that Christ and his disciple-apostles are represented on the streets of Rome by the two chief apostles, Peter and Paul.

In any case, there is no evidence that Irenaeus had pagan myths and legends in mind when he wrote about Peter and Paul founding the church of Rome. More research needs to be done to determine how early are the ideas like those of St. Leo the Great that Peter and Paul are "the fathers" of Rome comparable to, though of course more excellent than, Romulus and Remus.[1]

Nor is there any evidence that Tertullian had Romulus and Remus in mind by way of comparison as founders of Rome when he wrote that the apostles "poured their whole teaching along

with their blood" into the church of Rome (*Pre* 36.3). The reference would rather seem to be to the unique responsibility of the
apostles to "go and make disciples of all the Gentiles, teaching
them to observe all that I have commanded you" (Mt 28:20) and
to the dominical exhortation to martyrdom preserved in the
apostolic commission (Mt 10:16–22) and reemphasized in the
eschatological discourse of Jesus (Mt 24:9–14), which concludes
as follows:

> He who endures to the end will be saved. And this gos-
> pel of the kingdom will be preached throughout the
> whole world, as a testimony *(martyrion)* to all the
> nations; and then the end will come (vv. 13–14).

This means that the martyrdom of Peter and Paul is not for
Rome or for the Gentiles in Rome, in any restrictive sense, but
for all the nations throughout the whole world. The obedience of
Peter and Paul unto death is rendered in Rome, but it is for the
benefit of that whole world which God loved so much that he
gave his only begotten Son that all who believe in him might
have eternal life. Henceforth the city of Rome will provide a
locus for memorials to this crucial eschatological development at
the gravesites of these apostolic martyrdoms. With these two burial places functioning as the foci of an ecclesiastical elipsis shep-
herded by a single bishop, the church of Rome from henceforth
will be indeed a church to which Christians from everywhere can
come "with joy" to be "refreshed in the company of" God's
beloved in Rome (Rom 15:32), and in special instances missionaries can be sped on their way to preach the gospel "throughout
the whole world" (Mt 24:14). As such the church of Rome will
be an evangelical model for all churches. But no other church will
have said about it that it was founded by the apostles Peter and
Paul since these two chief apostles never rendered their obedience to the Gospel unto death in any other church. It is a bold
thesis. But it is better to state it without equivocation for the sake
of the discussion. By the church of Rome is meant the church of
the martyrs Peter and Paul. The Roman Catholic church neither
has nor claims to have any historical or theological grounds for

any special authority or service that can be based upon the nature or authority of the Christian community in Rome prior to the arrival in Rome of the apostles Peter and Paul.

As Kereszty has noted, the church of Rome is the custodian of the burial sites of the apostles Peter and Paul. It was also the primal traditioner of the living memory of the fact of their obedience unto death. All of the spiritual power that has come to Christians through the martyrdom of these apostles was experienced, appropriated, and traditioned in the first instance by the Christian community in Rome, which was transformed by these martyrdoms into "that very great, oldest, and well-known church" of which Irenaeus could say that it has always preserved the tradition coming from the apostles "for the faithful from everywhere."

It will be difficult at first to bear this distinction in mind because this "church of Rome" stands in very real continuity with the Christian community in Rome which already existed in Rome as the result of earlier preaching of the gospel, and already had a sufficient grasp of the gospel to be able to receive the martyrdoms of Peter and Paul and appropriate them faithfully for the benefit of Christians from everywhere. It is not to be imagined, however, that no other Christian community existed which could have received and appropriated these apostolic martyrdoms. One can only speculate on the consequences for church history had the apostles Peter and Paul been martyred in Antioch on the Orontes, meeting place of east and west. It is folly to deny the possibility that this might have expedited the preaching of the "gospel of the kingdom throughout the whole world" (Mt 24:14). It is equally foolish to speculate on "what might have been," except for the limited purpose of clarifying the grounds for attributing to the church of Rome a special place in the whole economy of the holy catholic church.

In this connection it is important to face the fact that, so far as we can tell, the joint martyrdom of Peter and Paul need not have taken place in the capital of the Roman empire. It might have taken place, and it might better have taken place, in Antioch. This is said without prejudice to Petrine claims based upon Matthew 16:13–19. There is, it should be noted, a tradition that

Peter was the first bishop of Antioch. Had Peter and Paul been martyred in Antioch, and had that church's community been able to receive and appropriate these martyrdoms for the benefit of Christians everywhere, so that thereafter "the faithful from everywhere" could have always found "the tradition coming from the apostles" preserved for them in and by that church, then there would have been a church of Antioch about which some second century theologian-bishop like Irenaeus might well have written:

> I can—by pointing out the tradition which that very great, oldest, and well-know church (founded and established at Antioch by those two most glorious apostles Peter and Paul) received from the apostles, and the faith she has announced to man, which comes down to us through the succession of bishops—put to shame all of those who in any way, either through wicked self-conceit, or through vainglory, or through blind and evil opinion, gather as they should not. For every church, that is, the faithful from everywhere must be in harmony with this church because of its most excellent origin, in which (church) the tradition coming from the apostles has always been preserved for the faithful from everywhere.

Another way to state the matter is to say that had not the apostles Peter and Paul founded and built up the church of Rome by pouring their whole teaching along with their blood into it, it would not have become "that very great, oldest, and well-known church," founded and established by "these two most glorious apostles," which Irenaeus knew and endorsed as "the church with which the faithful from everywhere must be in harmony." In conclusion, it appears that the case for according a special place for the church of Rome in the divine economy of the holy catholic church rests chiefly, if not entirely, upon "a theological assertion with some historical foundation" that in the providence of God the two most glorious apostles, Peter and Paul, poured their whole teaching and their blood into that church.[2]

This first part of my response to Kereszty's Chapter 4 appears to strengthen and explicate the convergence represented in our common recognition of the importance of the tradition that Peter and Paul founded the church of Rome, while at the same time it sharpens the distinction between this way of perceiving the special importance of the church of Rome and the stereotypical claims for the jurisdictional supremacy of the bishop of Rome from a particular understanding of Matthew 16:13–19, an interpretation of this scripture which has been and remains problem-causing for many Protestants.

"EARLIER GROUND FOR THE PRIMACY"

This leads us to take up Kereszty's attempt to argue a Roman Catholic case for what may be taken as the essential dogmatic teaching in the decrees on papal supremacy and infallibility. It should be borne in mind that Kereszty's attempt is not a fully developed systematic effort to do justice to these dogmatic decrees issued by the Vatican Council of 1870. Rather Kereszty's argument is concisely stated within the context of his effort to spell out the implications of his two theses for Roman Catholic systematic theology, the second of which reads as follows: "According to the New Testament and the early patristic view, the martyrdom of the two chief apostles is constitutive of the leadership role of the church of Rome."

Kereszty begins by reviewing evidence that makes clear that the joint importance of Peter and Paul has been recognized through the centuries. It is not just a second century phenomenon (pp. 82–84).

This is followed by a very important paragraph in which it is concluded that the attribution of "theological importance of the church of Rome to its being founded by the two martyred apostles Peter and Paul" cannot be said to be "merely a less perfect, provisional formulation of a later, more adequate doctrine." The "later" doctrine to which Fr. Kereszty refers is, of course, the dogma that "the bishop of Rome is the vicar (or in a nuanced sense the successor) of Peter" (p. 85). "The earlier ground for the primacy (i.e. that the two martyred apostles founded the church of Rome) is not based only upon the fact that its bishop is the vicar of Peter," that is, this "earlier ground for the primacy is not simply more primitive and less valid than the latter." In this way Kereszty rejects arguments which might be mounted to discount the importance of his two theses. Then comes a bold assertion: "The theological content of the first has not been adequately explicated by the second."

This assertion is then explained: "As in many cases of doctrinal development, a necessary refinement and articulation has been achieved at the expense of neglecting other aspects of a more encompassing truth of faith." In the first instance this is a Roman Catholic problem requiring the attention of Roman Catholic theologians working under the obligation of systematizing somewhat diverse traditions where a dogmatic decree based upon a later tradition stands in tension with an earlier tradition. It is nonetheless a theological discussion that not only is intrinsically interesting to Protestants but also appears to provide them some ground for hope that reaching an understanding, if not a total agreement, with Roman Catholic theologians may be more possible than has been thought.

Is it possible to go back behind a particular tradition upon which a dogmatic decree is based, or from which such a decree has developed, and there to find an earlier tradition which can be explicated in such a way as to alter the discussion of, and therefore, potentially, bring new understanding of, said dogmatic decree? If so, then, contrary to popular opinion, these Roman Catholic decrees often so troublesome for Protestants are no longer seen as set in concrete, as unchanging laws of the Medes and the Persians. Rather they can be viewed as living approximations of truth, reviewable, or at least capable of being understood within a more comprehensive context. New light can be thrown upon old questions by evidence uncovered by historians and theologians who are devoted to explicating the deposit of faith, especially as that deposit of faith is embodied in the church's canon, i.e. its holy scripture, and as embodied in the writings of these early Christian fathers of the church who were doing their work during the period of the history of the church when the church's New Testament canon was being formed.

PETER AND THE PAPACY?

We proceed to take up Kereszty's summary of the connection between Peter and the papacy. The focal point of the twofold dogmatic definition at Vatican I concerning the infallibility which the pope possesses under certain well-defined conditions and concerning his supreme immediate and universal jursidiction is summed up by Kereszty in a single sentence: "The church has gradually understood and defined at Vatican I that Peter received from Christ the mission to be the supreme visible center of unity for the church in matters of both doctrine and praxis" (p. 85). That Roman Catholic bishops under the leadership of the pope guided and supported above all by leading Jesuit theologians did in fact define at Vatican I certain decrees concerning the infallibility of the pope and his supreme and universal jurisdiction cannot be denied. But to say that "the church has gradually understood that Peter received from Christ the mission to be the supreme visible center of unity for the church in matters of both doctrine and praxis" would appear to beg the question.

NEW TESTAMENT EVIDENCE

Is this a gradual *understanding* or a gradual *misunderstanding* based upon a selective reading of the scriptures where words like "Get thee behind me, Satan. You are a stumbling block to me; for you are not on the side of God, but of men" (Mt 16:23), addressed by Jesus to Peter, are overlooked, or explained away? Such words do not support an understanding that Peter received from Christ the mission to be the supreme visible center of unity for the church, either in doctrine or in praxis. The harshness of this rebuke of Peter by Jesus is softened a little in the gospel according to Mark by the omission of the words: "You are a stumbling block to me" (Mk 8:33). But then this gospel also omits the pro-Petrine tradition found in the gospel of Matthew,

Blessed are you, Simon Bar-Jona. . . . Thou art Peter, and on this rock I will build my church, and the powers of hell shall not prevail against it. I will give you the keys

> of the kingdom of heaven, and whatever you bind on
> earth shall be bound in heaven, and whatever you loose
> on earth shall be loosed in heaven (Mt 16:17–19).

If one may judge by the arguments developed in the Vatican decrees of 1870, this scripture was foundational for the decree on the pope's relation to Peter and his supreme and universal jurisdiction and for the decree on the infallibility of the pope. Other scriptures are used for building up the arguments for these decrees, but none has the normative function that has Matthew 16:17–19. Within the New Testament, evidence bearing on the question of whether Peter received from Christ the mission to be the supreme visible center of unity for the church is inconclusive at best. Outside the New Testament, the earliest evidence that associates Peter with the church of Rome positions him alongside Paul, sharing equally in the founding and building of the church in Rome. In this earliest tradition it is Jesus Christ who is the supreme center of unity for the church in matters of both doctrine and praxis, and the chief apostles Peter and Paul receive from Christ through the Jerusalem apostles a dual mandate that Paul (and Barnabas) should go to the Gentiles, and Peter (and his associates) would go to the circumsized. The right hand of fellowship, given to Paul and Barnabas by the pillars of the Jerusalem church, Peter, James, and John, sealed the recognition that these pillars were united—visibly so—with Paul and Barnabas. They were united in preaching God's salvific love for all, both Jew and Gentile. It follows that if there ever was a single supreme visible center of unity for the church it would have been seen most clearly in that apostolic handshake in Jerusalem during the first ecumenical council of the church (Gal 2:1–10). To be sure, Peter, James, and John preceded Paul, and there is much New Testament evidence to suggest that Peter was the leading apostle among those who had worked directly with Jesus during that period of time when Jesus went in and out among his early disciples, beginning from the baptism of John until the ascension of Jesus (Acts 1:15–26). Any impartial reading of the New Testament will support the importance of Peter among the twelve. And that importance is supported by, if it is not rooted in, the tradition that Jesus as the risen Christ first appeared to Peter, then to the remainder of the twelve, before he appeared to over five hundred brethren at one time (1 Cor 15:3-6). Peter's primacy, according to this tradition, and in this restricted sense, extends over James the brother of Jesus, and over all the remaining apostles up to and including Paul (1 Cor 15:7-11).

It does not, however, in the same manner extend over the women mentioned in the gospel according to Matthew who went to see the place where Jesus was buried, and to whom Jesus first appeared (Mt 28:1-10). Since according to Roman law women at the time were not permitted to bear witness on such a matter in court, it is possible that the pre-Pauline tradition in 1 Corinthians 15:3-11 was developed along legal lines for maximum evidential force in early Christian evangelization.

In any case there is no convincing evidence, neither from the New Testament itself, nor from early fathers, to support the view that Peter "received from Christ the mission to be the supreme visible center of unity for the church both in matters of doctrine and praxis."

Therefore, when Kereszty proceeds to argue that "This center (i.e. Peter as the visible center of unity for the Church) must exist as long as the church does, until the end of human history" (p. 85) he is engaged in a theological argument whose cogency is by no means self-evident. Here we have an item to be placed on our agenda for further research and discussion. Some of the questions to be researched can be stated thus: How, in fact, did the relevant decrees of Vatican I develop? What light can be thrown upon the origin of the tradition linking Peter with the bishop of Rome? What did the Protestant reformers write on this and related topics? They had been Roman Catholics and presumably received Catholic teaching as it had developed to their time. Did they know the tradition that the church of Rome was founded by Peter *and* Paul? How was their reliance upon the apostle Paul related to Roman Catholic teaching about the pope as the vicar of Christ? Did the counter-reformation influence the subsequent development of the Vatican decrees of 1870?

When Kereszty writes: "However if we search for the actual existence of this center (i.e. Peter as the supreme visible center of unity) we find historical evidence only for the church of Rome which early tradition considers to have been founded by Peter and Paul," he points up the problem we face. Only the church of Rome is associated with the tradition of Peter as the supreme visible center of unity for the church. But why is this? Why not the church of Jerusalem where Peter was the chief of the twelve? Why not the church of Antioch whose first bishop Peter may have been? Why the church of Rome since early tradition considers it to have been founded by Peter *and* Paul?

There are two questions to ask: (1) Why is there any association at all between Peter and the church of Rome? (2) Why, when Peter is associated with the founding of the church of Rome, is he represented as a co-founder with Paul? Regarding the first question, we can observe that while the first epistle of Peter obliquely associates the name of the apostle Peter with the city of Rome (under the code name Babylon), it is Peter's martyrdom that links him to the church in Rome more strongly than to the church in any other city. And similarly, in considering the second question, we note that when Peter's name is mentioned in connection with the founding of the church of Rome, it is mentioned along with that of Paul as a co-founder because their joint founding of the church of Rome flows from or is perceived as a consequence of their joint martyrdom in that city.

These considerations serve to further strengthen the view that if there was a supreme visible center of unity for the church in matters of both doctrine and praxis in the period following the fall of Jerusalem in A.D. 70, and the scattering of the Jerusalem apostles from this original apostolic center, it would have been the visible markers of the graves of the martyred apostles Peter and Paul in Rome. It was here that those two apostolic heads of the twofold apostolic mission to Jews and Gentiles, leaders who had earlier given and received the right hand of apostolic fellowship in Jerusalem in the conference which had given birth to this apostolic joint mission, subsequently rejoined one another in giving apostolic consolation and inspiration to the Christian community in Rome in a time of persecution. Here they had poured the whole of their mutual apostolic teaching "along with their blood" into the church (Tertullian, *Pre* 36.3). Here the right hand of fellowship given in Jerusalem was institutionalized and made visible.

PATRISTIC EVIDENCE

As is suggested by Kereszty in Chapter 3 (pp. 65-69), it would appear to follow that the Roman bishops' awareness of having the power to exclude local churches from the communion of a universal church, which awareness Kereszty traces back as early as bishop Victor at the end of the second century, was related to these bishops' episcopal care of the church founded by the martyred apostles Peter and Paul. We may add that it would have been an essential duty of every bishop of Rome, after the martyrdom of these apostles, to provide for the maintenance of, and to adjudicate all local disputes over care of and access to, these two apostolic gravesites.

In visiting these sites, compliance with regulations ultimately approved by the bishop of Rome would have been expected of the faithful from everywhere. This compliance would have been given out of love for and gratitude to the church of Rome. For by common consent it would have been recognized by the faithful from everywhere that the church of Rome, out of love and respect for Peter and Paul, had the responsibility to offer hospitality to pilgrims and to that end regulate such visitation. This is the best and most concrete way in which to illustrate how jurisdictional primacy for the bishop of Rome effectuated itself as a practical consequence of the martyrdoms of the apostles Peter and Paul. There is nothing mysterious about it in the first instance. The principle may be simply stated. The priest is in charge of the funeral and oversees the treatment of the dead. Visitation to burial sites comes under the ultimate jurisdiction of the priest in charge. That priest, certainly in the case of the burial sites of the apostles, was under the supervision of the bishop of Rome or his designate.

The faithful from everywhere would have accepted the jurisdiction of the bishop of Rome over the burial sites of the apostles with the expectation that he would exercise his authority out of love and in the spirit of a martyrological tradition exemplified by

Jesus and represented in Rome on behalf of the faithful from everywhere by Peter and Paul. They would have expected the bishop of this church to exercise all his authority in the spirit of that mutual apostolic teaching these apostles poured into the church with their blood. In turn they would have expected their own bishops to be in harmony with the bishop of this the local church of the city of Rome. We may imagine that in many instances their own bishop would be leading the pilgrimage and any prior or subsequent meeting with the bishop of Rome in the company of their bishop would have been a high moment. It is intrinsically probable that in some instances a eucharistic meal would have been shared. If and when these meals took place in close relationship to or at the actual site of the burial of one of the apostles and especially if the bishop of Rome and a visiting bishop were both participating in the commemorative worship service, the faithful would have been especially conscious of the meaning of participation in the life of the holy catholic church. Only the experience of martyrdom itself could have exceeded in significance such immediate participation in the mystery of the faith of the holy catholic church.

Under these circumstances the power to exclude local churches from the communion of the holy catholic church would have resided in the consciousness of the faithful that in the church of Rome they could find the living tradition of the apostles always preserved for the faithful from everywhere. Whenever, and to the extent that, that proved not to be the case, the power of the bishop of Rome to exclude local churches from the communion of the holy catholic church would be adversely affected. Moreover, whenever this power to exclude was abused, the faithful from anywhere through their local bishop could effectively call into question such abuse. This is precisely what happened when the bishop of Rome excluded the churches from Asia Minor from communion over the issue of fixing the date of Easter. It must have been a cause of inconvenience and possibly a cause of considerable ecclesiastical confusion for Christians from Asia Minor residing in Rome not to observe Easter together with "the faithful from everywhere" according to a *common* ecclesiastical calendar. And yet it was possible for the bishop of the church in the Rhone Valley in Gaul to write his fellow bishop of the church in Rome and successfully remonstrate with him over this abuse of the power to exclude. Thus the power to exclude was not absolute, and the bishop of Rome could be held accountable to scripture and tradition by bishops of other local churches.

In fact, the faithful from everywhere had a special relationship to the local bishop of Rome that entitled them through their local bishop to remonstrate with him when necessary, even in matters affecting other local churches more directly than their own. To be sure, this may not have happened often, but the reason for that is given by Irenaeus himself: "the faithful from everywhere must be in harmony with the church of Rome because of its most excellent origin, i.e. founded and established by those two most glorious apostles, Peter and Paul." What Irenaeus did in remonstrating with the bishop of Rome over that bishop's exclusion from communion (with the church of Rome) of churches in Asia Minor was to focus attention on how this threatened act (on the part of the bishop of Rome) would not be in harmony with the tradition of the church of Rome. It would have been an action inconsistent with a previous action by a previous bishop of Rome in a similar case and, by implication, not in harmony with the ecclesiology of the holy catholic church.

To state, as Kereszty does, that the power to exclude, beginning with bishop Victor at the end of the second century, "is the historical basis on which the Catholic dogma of Petrine succession rests," calls for further research. Kereszty himself in Chapter 3 states that "Victor may have derived his authority for excommunicating entire churches not from any Petrine text of the New Testament but from the tombs and presence of the martyr apostles Peter and Paul" (p. 67).

"THE UNITY OF THE CHURCH"

For Kereszty to go on to write in Chapter 4 that "as bishop of Rome, the pope succeeds to Peter in the sense that Peter continues through the pope his ministry for the unity of the church" (p. 85) is not compelling. The relative deemphasis of Petrine primacy in Vatican II in comparison to Vatican I appears to have better served the church's need for unity. Pope John seemed to Protestants, or at least to Protestants who appreciated the council he called, to make no claim for himself nor for his council that called for any stress on a concept of Petrine succession, let alone papal supremacy or infallibility. And the present pope, with his many journeys to far distant places, is as much a representative of the apostle to the Gentiles as he is a successor to the prince of the apostles. It is true that in the liturgy for his installation as Pope which took place in Piazza di San Pietro, John Paul was repeatedly told by the assembled faithful that he was Peter. However, "You are Peter" is set in the liturgy of installation and is required by tradition. Similarly, it is true that when it is used liturgically the text of Matthew 16:13–19 has a profound ontic significance for many if not all Roman Catholics. However, where freedom is allowed and tradition does not determine the outcome, the present bishop of Rome appears to live and function out of a consciousness of his responsibility to show forth the Roman Catholic church's obligation to represent the whole teaching of the apostles without restriction.

PETRINE SUCCESSION

The present pope is serving as a visible center of unity for the church. But in the perception of Protestants he serves as this visible center as much in spite of Roman Catholic stress on Petrine succession as because of Roman Catholic adherence to this doctrine. I see no intrinsic reason or compelling need for Roman Catholics to emphasize or even argue for Petrine succession. The special importance of the church of Rome does not appear to me to require Petrine succession—at least not as Irenaeus perceived this importance. All that has been said here in response to what Kereszty has said in Chapter 4 on these matters is in accordance with and supported by what Kereszty has written in Chapter 3, "The Church of Rome and the Easter Controversy from the Viewpoint of Irenaeus" (pp. 65–69). Similarly, there are some things that have been added in this response that converge with and serve to strengthen Kereszty's conclusion given at the end of his treatment of Irenaeus in Chapter 3, "The normativity of the church of Rome for all the other churches is not based on any Petrine text of the New Testament but rather on its joint foundation by the two most important martyr apostles Peter and Paul" (p 68).

There is no intrinsic Protestant objection to emphasizing the importance of the Petrine heritage in the holy catholic church. But Protestants are disposed by scripture and their Protestant tradition to think of every Christian having equal access to that heritage and presently see no reason to accord to the bishop of Rome a greater responsibility to protect, guard and increase this Petrine heritage in the church than she or he would accord to any other bishop, or, for that matter, to any other theologian or leader of the church. This is chiefly because Protestants in the main remain unpersuaded by arguments in behalf of claims for Petrine succession in the Roman Catholic church. But on this point Protestants may be wrong. I am not persuaded that they are, but I acknowledge the possibility. The matter is certainly worthy of further study, reflection, and research.

"PETER AND PAUL" AND PRIMACY

In the meantime the early tradition that the church of Rome was founded and built up by the apostles Peter *and* Paul, and that these apostles poured their whole teaching along with their blood into the church while it was being persecuted in the city of Rome, provides an historical and theological basis for Protestants to reassess whether or not in fact the church of Rome and therefore its bishop might not, on some other basis than Petrine succession, have a special responsibility to preserve and actualize in every age the Petrine heritage, including the heritage to shepherd, to reconcile, and to unify the church. In this case, however, it would be no less the responsibility of the bishop of Rome to preserve and actualize in every age the Pauline heritage of an evangelical mission to all nations and of a doctrinal and practical concern for the truth of the gospel.

According to ecumenical protocol, in any future council involving the patriarchs of orthodox churches and the judicatory heads of other churches including the church of Rome, the bishop of Rome would enter the council chamber first, on the grounds that he is "first in love." Protestants should be reasonably open to such practical implications of this way of according some measure of primacy to the bishop of Rome. It is a primacy that is commensurate with the role of the bishop of Rome when he is representing the interests and heritage of the martyred apostles Peter and Paul.

For Protestants the bishop of Rome cannot automatically or in principle be first in jurisdiction out of the heritage of Peter alone. But he might be first out of the heritage of Peter *and* Paul. It is conceivable that he could be accepted in this way by Protestants were they encouraged to perceive him as standing, as bishop of Rome, under a unique obligation to be foremost in love and truth, and in this moral sense foremost in jurisdiction, as a foremost servant of the Lord.

These extended comments on Kereszty's attempt to preserve a significant measure of importance for the traditional one-sided Roman Catholic emphasis upon the importance of Peter for the church are in some sense gratuitous, since Kereszty is performing an essential task in Roman Catholic systematic theology. He cannot reject the Roman Catholic doctrine of Petrine succession. He must state the case for it fairly in a form that can be appropriated and affirmed by Roman Catholic theologians. But this theological exercise is made necessary by the more urgent need to focus the attention of Roman Catholic theologians upon implications for Catholic systematic theology of the recognition that the bishop of Rome is "called to be an heir no less to Paul than to Peter" (p. 87). It would seem to follow from what Kereszty says under this head that the bishop of Rome must indirectly exercise his unique but widely unacknowledged apostolic responsibility to and for the whole church through advisements, persuasion, exhortation and example, while directly exercising his acknowledged episcopal authority over the church of Rome and over those in direct communion with that very great, oldest, and well-known church.

A Protestant would want to affirm that any bona fide primacy of Rome is an epiphenomenon of the primacy of the apostolic faith poured out with their blood into the church of Rome by Peter and Paul. This apostolic faith is grounded in the atoning sacrifice of Jesus Christ made in Jerusalem for all humankind. The benefits of this sacrifice for the nations were providentially and exponentially expedited by the apostolic suffering and martyrdom of Peter and Paul in Rome, which suffering powerfully served to complete the suffering of Christ for the salvation of the world. All who stand in this tradition (which is the particular Christian tradition witnessed to in the church's New Testament and confirmed by the tradition of the apostolic fathers and the subsequent fathers of the second century church, a tradition inextricably bound up with both Jerusalem and Rome) are called upon to complete the sufferings of Christ as did Peter and Paul. This is the apostolic faith of the holy catholic church which has formed the New Testament for the faithful. In that church, the church of Rome has a primacy grounded in history as interpreted by faith in the light of scripture. That primacy can find expression in an infinite variety of forms, some authentic and some demonic. No church is immune from the corrupting influence of sin. And the very primacy of Rome of which we are speaking makes the church of Rome and its bishops especially vulnerable to the wiles of Satan. This vulnerability, however, is not unique. It is shared by the faithful from everywhere and by every church whether or not it is in harmony with the church of Rome.

When, however, this apostolic faith, by God's grace, and with the assistance of his Holy Spirit, is given authentic expression, the purpose of God in sending his Servant into the world to save the nations is being fulfilled. The faithful, especially those who are faithful unto death, participate in God's kingdom made real in the life, death, burial, and exaltation of Jesus Christ.

THE PRESENCE OF PETER AND PAUL
IN THE CHURCH OF ROME

The major difference between the above (Protestant?) way of understanding the significance of the martyrdoms of Peter and Paul in Rome for systematic theology and that spelled out by Kereszty in his discussion of the implications of these martyrdoms for Roman Catholic systematic theology centers in the doctrine that Peter and Paul are present in a special way in the church of Rome. Kereszty points out that according to Roman Catholic belief, the apostles Peter and Paul intercede for the church of Rome "and thereby rule and protect it" (p. 84).

The cult of the apostles is notably absent in most if not all forms of contemporary Protestantism. It is a matter worthy of further study, reflection, and research to determine how and why this is so. Presumably Luther inherited some belief in the continuing activity of the apostles in the life of the church. If so, no doubt such belief in some circles was bound up with elements that were inauthentic and possibly demonic and may have cried out for reform in his own time and place. But the question of whether such belief that Peter and Paul and martyrs in general can be present with Christians in moments of faith should be regarded as valid or as invalid is a matter requiring serious reflection and further research into the meaning and reality of Christian worship. If there is a sense in which these martyrs can be present in contemporary Christian worship, or if there is a sense in which they were believed to be present in the worship experience of that early pre-Constantinian church which has given us our New Testament, then contemporary Protestant, Roman Catholic, and Orthodox theologians have a potentially fruitful topic on which to reflect as they work to strengthen and extend that unity which is calling into being and promises to nurture the coming great church.

From a Protestant perspective the doctrine of the real presence of Christ in the eucharist can take on added meaning if Christ is experienced as present not in isolation from, but surrounded by, his martyred apostles. The gospel teaching that where two or three of the faithful are gathered together in the name of Jesus he will be present in their midst can be enriched if Christians are also enabled by faith to experience the presence of martyrs for the faith from among their own community, as is the case today among Christians in many parts of the world, e.g., in Central America. There is thus a basis, if not in scripture, then in reason and Christian experience, for Protestants to begin the theological adventure of enriching their faith through reflection upon and reappropriation of neglected but valid elements from their catholic heritage.[3]

It is reasonable to expect that if this reflection upon a common heritage, especially that coming from the early church, were carried out on a basis of confessional mutuality, theologians would be in a better position to distinguish between developments of doctrines that are to be judged valid, and any that may be judged to stand in need of reformation. Whether in this process of academic colleagueship, observing the principle of confessional mutuality, a meaningful convergence of views between Roman Catholics and Protestants would emerge remains to be seen. No doubt, participation of Orthodox theologians in the discussion, providing it takes place in a meaningful manner and at a meaningful time, would improve the possibility of any such convergence having lasting value.

Chapter Six

FURTHER CONVERGENCE WITH CONTINUING DIFFERENCES OVER COLLEGIALITY

In the process of writing this book, we found more common ground than is summarized in the jointly written opening chapter, but, as our discussions progressed, we could also perceive the remaining differences between our positions more clearly than before. In this last chapter we shall formulate both this new common ground and our more clearly understood differences.

BASIC DIFFERENCES

Farmer sees the relationship between Peter and Paul as full and complete mutuality and finds no foundation in the New Testament for even the beginnings of a "Petrine primacy" over Paul. In fact, he is inclined to think that, besides being the first witness to the risen Christ, any further prominence above the other "pillars" of the Jerusalem church accrues to Peter primarily because of his leading role in responding to God's call for the apostles to engage in the evangelization of the Gentiles (Acts 10:1–11:18), and with the closely related connection he had with Paul as attested in Galatians 1:18–24. Peter, it would appear, recognized Paul's call to preach the gospel to the Gentiles and accepted Paul's gospel as a valid version of the gospel of Christ more readily than the other Jerusalem apostles, in particular James. Peter appears to have been first and foremost among the twelve to advocate cooperation with Paul. Thus, the importance of Peter among the early apostles, Farmer believes, has been linked to his role of mediator between Paul and those in Jerusalem who had been apostles before him. Therefore, any attempt to base a doctrine of the primacy of the bishop of Rome for the universal church on an alleged Petrine succession alone appears to Farmer as lacking both scriptural and historical evidence. Yet Farmer is inclined to see a providential role for the bishop of Rome on the grounds that this bishop is heir in a special sense of both martyr apostles, Peter and Paul.

While agreeing that Peter was more open to the special call of Paul than was James and that Peter may have acted as a mediator between James and Paul, Kereszty is convinced that Peter's importance and leadership role ultimately rests on his special call by Christ. This, Kereszty believes, is sufficiently attested by the cumulative evidence of the synoptic gospels. Moreover, Kereszty thinks that the fourth gospel was accepted in the universal church only with an appendix that claims for Peter the Christ-given role to represent the good shepherd for the universal church. The last document of the New Testament, 2 Peter, implies that Peter holds the key to the right interpretation of Paul whose God-inspired wisdom and writings the author of 2 Peter accepts. Thus, Kereszty believes that the twofold Roman Catholic dogma regarding the bishop of Rome, who as successor of Peter has supreme and full power of jurisdiction over the universal Church and who shares in the charism given to the church for teaching the deposit of faith infallibly under some definite conditions, has a sufficient scriptural basis.[1] Yet he is also convinced that this Roman Catholic dogma needs to be integrated into the larger truth attested by both scripture and the uninterrupted tradition of the church that "the bishop of Rome is an heir no less to Paul than to Peter."

CONVERGENCE ON COLLEGIALITY

On this limited yet real commonality, we now make one further step and formulate together what may follow from the common relationship of the bishop of Rome to Peter and Paul for his role regarding the universal church. We should start with the undeniable fact that (regardless of how we further determine their relationship) Peter and Paul became partners in the Lord both in their apostolic missions and in their martyr deaths, and that, after their martyrdom, the memory of their partnership proved to be a decisive force in determining the importance of the church of Rome, in shaping the life and structure of catholic Christianity and thus in the shaping of the scriptural canon. Their partnership—or, to use a theological term, their collegial relationship—is the sign and the result of the agreement of the larger collegial group in Jerusalem, James and John, Peter, Paul and Barnabas (Gal 2:1–10), while the Jerusalem handshake of fellowship is the sign and the effective means of realizing the collegial unity of all the apostles of Jesus Christ. Thus, one of the most important consequences of the permanently attested fact that the bishop of Rome claims to act "by the authority of Peter and Paul" is the collegial nature of his authority.

This authority is collegial in origin, collegial in its exercise, and collegial in its goal. It is collegial in origin because he is the heir of not only one apostle, but of both Peter and Paul, and through them of the whole apostolic college. That his authority is collegial in its goal means that all the actions of teaching and leading on the part of the bishop of Rome should aim at preserving and promoting the unity of all the local churches whose communion makes up the one holy catholic church of Christ. Thus he ought to use his authority as a ministry of universal service. He should not domineer over the other local churches (cf. 1 Pet 5:3), but rather try to assure that all local churches are equally a church of Christ, in the purity of faith, in the evangelical way of life and in church polity. With Gregory I, he should feel truly honored when due honor is paid to all the local churches and their bishops. In Gregory's words, "My honor is the honor of the universal church. My honor is the solid strength of my brothers (in the episcopal dignity)."[2]

DISAGREEMENT ON THE RELATIONSHIP OF THE BISHOP OF ROME TO THE REST OF THE EPISCOPACY

While we were able to find common language in describing the collegial nature, origin and goal of the ministry of the bishop of Rome, we are still far apart when facing the relationship of the bishop of Rome to the rest of the episcopacy. On the one hand, Kereszty believes the Catholic tradition as formulated in *Lumen Gentium* of Vatican II: the bishop of Rome is the head of the episcopal college in such a way that, without him, the college as such does not exist, and, without his approval or consent, it cannot validly act, while the bishop of Rome can, at his discretion, act freely and validly without the actual cooperation of the college.[3] Kereszty is also convinced that such freedom of action, if understood correctly, does not contradict the collegial nature of papal authority. Moreover, Kereszty believes that this freedom of action has proved providential several times in the history of the church, not the least significant instance being the convocation of Vatican II by John XXIII and the energetic and diplomatic interventions of Paul VI during the sessions of the council. Without the free initiatives of these two popes the renewal and reforms of Vatican II could not have taken place, nor would the overwhelming majority of Roman Catholic bishops and faithful have accepted these reforms if they had not believed in the primacy of the bishop of Rome.

Farmer, on the other hand, is of the opinion that this Roman Catholic formulation on the freedom of action of the bishop of Rome constitutes an almost insurmountable obstacle to reunion. How can Protestants (and Farmer presumes that the Orthodox would certainly concur with the Protestants in this matter) forget the gradual transformation of the authority of Rome from a last instance of appeal to a more and more centralized form of government, a government which has also accumulated more and more secular power into its hands and ended up by becoming corrupt itself and spreading corruption throughout the entire church? At one point in Jesus' earthly ministry, Peter deserved to be called Satan by Jesus himself. Throughout the church's history, some of the popes were even more successful than Peter in becoming the instruments of Satan. Thus, allowing for an unchecked freedom of papal power is the surest way to compromise the integrity of ecclesiastical authority at the highest level. There is a need for strong leadership in the church but it must be based on a collegial consensus. Popes John XXIII and Paul VI, even when they acted on their own initiative, still expressed and articulated the aspirations and the faith of the universal church. Moreover, the Protestant and Orthodox observers at the council were included in the consultation process and effectively contributed to the form and content of the conciliar documents. This is one of the reasons why many Protestants take so seriously the teachings of Vatican II.

While unable to agree on how to overcome the difference of belief on the relationship of the bishop of Rome to the other bishops we still agreed on a list of considerations, one to be reflected upon by Roman Catholics, another by Protestants, which, while not yet creating a consensus, may narrow the gap.

PROPOSED CONSIDERATIONS FOR CATHOLICS

1.   On the basis of what was said before, even the personal official acts of the bishop of Rome must be considered collegial acts since, whenever he acts in his official capacity, he always acts as head of the college and is bound by the whole apostolic heritage and especially that of Peter and Paul. He is not free to deviate from the apostolic faith and from the apostolic way of life, nor may he discard the apostolic institutions. In his teaching he is to proclaim, explain and defend the faith of the church, not his own personal opinions.

2.   In the exercise of his teaching ministry, he has the moral obligation (the more solemn the manner of teaching, the graver the obligation) to consult with the universal church to ascertain that he indeed articulates the apostolic faith of the church. Yet it is hardly possible to determine a priori for each case the manner and the extent required for the consultation.

3.   With regard to intervening in the life of a local church (the exercise of his universal supreme jurisdiction) Roman Catholics should indeed keep in mind that the present system of centralized papal authority did not yet exist in the patristic age. During that time the bishop of Rome intervened in other local churches only as a final arbiter when the local churches could not or would not resolve an issue which threatened the unity of the

universal church in matters of faith, morals or church polity. When Roman Catholics look for that "minimum" implicit belief in papal primacy which would satisfy the Roman Catholic dogma, they should base their formulation on this long historic experience of both the western and eastern churches. The primacy of the bishop of Rome is acknowledged if communion with the church of Rome (communion in faith, sacramental life and ministry) is accepted as constitutive of communion with the holy Catholic Church of God. It seems that in case of an eventual reunion this alone is that non-negotiable minimum required by the self-identity of the Roman Catholic church. In what concrete ways and forms this communion is to be realized should be worked out in a dialogue which keeps in mind two theological principles: on the one hand every local church gathered around her bishop is a true realization of the church of Christ and thus a "sister" church of Rome which deserves respect and autonomy; on the other hand, the charism of the bishop of Rome is to safeguard the communion of all local churches by assuring the conditions of unity. If we examine the relationship of Rome to the Oriental churches already in communion with Rome, and especially the development of that relationship after Vatican II, we may find many signs which show that the church of Rome respects and safeguards the eastern traditions in liturgy, theology and church polity. These provide some guidelines for possible future cases of reunion.

4.   On balance, looking at the whole span of the history of the church, the church of Rome, in the words of Paul Tillich, has still preserved the "Catholic substance," the substance, that is, of apostolic faith.

Yet, in that preservation, the papacy was only one factor, supported and counterbalanced in various ways by the bishops, and theologians, but more importantly by the saints coming from clergy and laity alike as well as by the whole people of God.

5.   Loyal criticism of the pope and of the Roman curia has played an important role in the process of preserving and renewing the apostolic heritage of the church of Rome. Roman Catholics would do well to read the frank and serious charges that saints like Bernard of Clairvaux and Catherine of Siena leveled

against certain actions of the pope. It is as true today as it has always been: if a Christian is sincerely convinced that a pope teaches what is not the faith of the church and intervenes in the life of a local church in such a way as to cause scandal or provokes a schism unnecessarily, other conditions being observed,[4] he cannot call the papal actions invalid, yet he has the moral right and obligation to speak his conscience and even openly criticize the actions of the pope while being ready to admit that he may be misinformed or wrong in his criticism.

While the above points summarize a long Roman Catholic tradition, they are not widely known. It may be helpful for Roman Catholics to become more aware that such "limits" on the pope's power do exist and have always existed within the Roman Catholic tradition.

PROPOSED CONSIDERATIONS FOR PROTESTANTS

Before Protestants definitively exclude the possibility of any legitimate authoritative action on the part of the bishop of Rome in a local church, they would do well to reflect on two issues.

1. They should consider the way the apostle Paul handled the churches he had founded. He would plead with his faithful as a mother and father, yet when everything else failed he did not hesitate to make the whole weight of his apostolic authority felt in giving norms for the eucharistic life (1 Cor 10–11), marriages (1 Cor 7), lawsuits in the church in Corinth (1 Cor 6), and excommunication of an incestuous man "in the name of our Lord Jesus Christ" and with his "power" (1 Cor 5:4). Contrary to a widespread stereotype, Paul is documented by the New Testament to have acted more often with an authority which did not admit of any further appeal than is Peter, who was actually rebuked by Paul for compromising with the Judaizers on "the right way of life according to the truth of the gospel" (cf. Gal 2:11–14). If we allow a bishop only the right to plead and exhort but deny his right to act with authority, "the freedom we have in Christ Jesus" may be turned into a cover for the hubris of unredeemed humanity which will undermine "the obedience of faith."

2. The apostolic faith laid down in the New Testament and

the united witness of Peter and Paul in particular are not a dead letter but the living word of God destined to address every new historical situation, to judge and comfort, to give light and guidance in every new cultural context. Just repeating the biblical message word by word would leave it irrelevant and even incomprehensible for modern humanity. Hence a need arises for a constant "translation" and interpretation. The time may have come for Protestants to take a second look at the interpreting activity of the church of Rome. If they find more and more evidence that the church of Rome intends to be faithful to the whole of the New Testament, that is, both the Petrine and Pauline heritage (and also the whole apostolic faith including the Johannine writings), perhaps a way may be found for Protestants to regard full communion with the church of Rome as mutually desirable if not indispensable for the sake of the Holy Catholic Church.

Many important topics in this area, we admit, were not even touched upon, and those treated were not exhausted. We are also aware that any effective treatment of collegiality asks for the inclusion of Orthodox dialogue partners. We only hope to have made a small step toward building a consensus in restating the collegial relationship of the martyr apostles Peter and Paul.

EPILOGUE

Readers who have come thus far in this remarkable little book will almost certainly have had a few questions raised for them about its venue and context. It is not yet commonplace to come across fresh and insightful discussions of a basic ecumenical problem and to have it reviewed historically and probed ecumenically by a pair of scholars from disparate fields of inquiry and from different traditions. The senior partner in this particular venture is a well-known New Testament scholar (an American already distinguished for his pioneering work in the current re-openings of "The Synoptic Problem"). His junior partner is a seasoned patrologist and theologian (a Roman Catholic, a Hungarian, and a Cistercian monk into the bargain). The critical reader will already have formed a judgment as to their evidence and arguments, and I hope that most of them will have agreed with me that the joint product is truly competent, genuinely dialogical and evocative of fruitful insights. They will have sensed the distinctive spirit of the inquiry: it is objective without being detached; it is accessible both to experts and to the general reader. It is candid without being contentious; it bears no marks of partisan zeal on either side even as it nudges back the horizons of a problem that has puzzled and plagued the Christian community from its beginnings.

Its further importance, I think, is that it represents a fair sampling of what is now being spoken of increasingly as "ecumenical church history." This is a phrase for the sort of church history that is cast in the mode and measured by the standards of critical historiography in general, but that consciously distinguishes itself from the adversarial spirit and tempers that we have seen in rival denominational histories since *The Centuries* of Magdeburg and the answering *Annales* of Baronius. Ecumenical church history is less concerned with a formula for recovered

130

Christian unity than it is with an historical understanding of the actual circumstances and interests of Christians in agreement and disagreement, over the course of the centuries and across the wide bounds of space and cultural diversity. It presupposes that shared historical understanding will aid in the cause of Christian unity indirectly. But its direct concern is more with credible narratives than with triumphalist demonstrations.

This sort of church history, of course, is not new. It came with the rise of modern historical consciousness in the 18th and 19th centuries, reflected in the work of such great summators as von Ranke, Dilthey and Troeltsch. Its specific implications for the cause of Christian unity were lifted up in Lund (1952) at the Third World Conference of Faith and Order, in the discussions there of "our common history as Christians"—i.e., the still potent memories of a Christian tradition that is longer, richer and more truly "catholic" than any denominational slicing of it. Crucial in such a perspective are ideas such as "identity," "continuity," and "development" in and through the successive cultural crises through which Christianity has passed. Guiding visions of how such ideas have informed "our Christian memory" are reflected in the groundbreaking work of such church historians as Yves-Marie Congar, Georges Florovsky and Jaroslav Pelikan. The American Society of Church History has recently established an award for "outstanding contributions to ecumenical church history, broadly conceived."

The aim of such history looks beyond mere tolerance and amity towards truly mutual respect and recognition between Christians, but also beyond this to critically accountable dialogue and disciplined inquiry that may stimulate and guide further inquiry and deeper understanding. Ecumenical church history rejects, out of hand, any conscious compromise of conscience; it welcomes full candor from all participants. It scorns appeals to arbitrary authority and relies upon persuasion as the energy of any valid consensus.

As I can certify, both of the partners in this particular dialogue are already veterans in this newer form of historical analysis and interpretation. The three of us have belonged to a regional faculty seminar that has been working together now in central Texas for two decades, (a sort of by-product of the Second Vatican Council!). It has included ranking scholars from ten different academic institutions. They, in their turn, have represented at least that many different traditions. Among them, they constitute a broad spectrum of American Christianity (Eastern Orthodox excepted). None of them, however, has had any official portfolio from his or her tradition.

Our bracketed field of historical inquiry (i.e., "the Development of catholic Christianity in the Second Century") was carefully chosen for a cluster of different reasons. In the first place, of course, the second century has a special interest and importance all its own as the crucial bridge epoch between Christianity's emergence from within its Jewish matrix and its subsequent stabilizations in a Hellenistic culture within the Roman Empire (as an *ecclesia* rather than another *thiasos*). But also it presents itself as a relatively level playing field on which New Testament experts, church historians *and* theologians can improve their skills. A sort of shared competence has been required of us all but there are no experts who can dominate our discussions (after all, the second century is one of the most scantily documented of all the truly crucial epochs in church history). Third, such a field has allowed us to proceed with our cumulative inquiries, without any prior commitment to some single ecumenical model in the contemporary scene. This has had the effect of encouraging more actual ecumenical *experience* than any agenda aimed directly at ecclesiological consensus could ever have done. On principle, we left open the questions of *termini ad quem* for New Testament students *or* any precise *terminus a quo* for the church historians. The result has been a sort of makeshift bridge over the hermeneutical chasms that have yawned between New Testament studies and patristics for too long. In the early years, the seminar adopted a provisional agenda: a sort of survey of the epoch between Domitian and the Severans. Over the years, and rather unexpectedly, it evolved into something more like an archaeological dig, with basic reference points along a continuum stretching from the primal origins to the ecumenical creeds and to the councils. Moreover, during the whole protracted experience, and despite our wide variegations, I cannot remember a paper that violated our tacit taboo against triumphalism.

It is against a background such as this that I have found *Peter and Paul in the Church of Rome* a very gratifying contribution. Its spirit is concordant; its expositions reflect honest agreements and disagreements. There are no easy harmonizings and its conclusions illumine fiercely controverted issues with a calmer, clearer light. The study begins with an effort to make sense of the unvarnished accounts in the New Testament of the ambivalent relationships between Sts. Peter and Paul: the apostolic claims of St. Paul, the meanings and importance of their exchange of "the right hand of fellowship" in Jerusalem (Galatians 2:9), their subsequent missions in Rome and their concurrent martyrdoms there in the Neronian persecutions. The Protestant professor and the Roman Catholic monk find that the evidence allows them to speak of the two great apostles as "heads of two separate but concordant missions" whose partnership "was reaffirmed martyrologically by their signatures in blood." This theme of shared leadership in the "Catholic Church" *(kata ten holen)* is further developed by second- and third-century leaders as like and unlike as St. Irenaeus, Tertullian and Origen. And Fr. Kereszty reminds us of the tradition being set in formulary style by Pope Nicholas I (in a letter to the Byzantine emperor!) where the pope speaks *per auctoritatem Apostolorum Petri et Pauli.* While agreeing with Farmer on the normative importance of the partnership of Peter and Paul, Kereszty disassociates himself to some extent from his Protestant colleague by affirming that the beginnings of a "petrine" primacy over the universal church can be found in a canonical reading of the New Testament. Nevertheless, he points to the complementary roles of the two chief apostles and even to the superiority of Paul over Peter as a missionary and inspired theologian.

This essay has helped me to understand the deeper symbolism of those two larger-than-life statues of Sts. Peter and Paul in the Piazza San Pietro, where in that magnificent space defined by the Bernini Colonnade, St. Paul stands forth as the personification of the contemplative life, whereas St. Peter is as clearly the divinely appointed CEO of the church mundane. It also prompted a guess that some such understanding prompted Pope Paul VI to set the closing service of shared prayer and worship at the Second Vatican Council (between the Pope and bishops, and the "delegated observers"), in the basilica of St. Paul's-outside-the-Walls. Fr. Kereszty reminds us how in Christian iconography, St. Paul is often seated at the risen Christ's "right hand," and how, in both Roman and Byzantine liturgies, it is Christ himself who is *the* Rock on which the church stands, with St. Peter and his successors as earthly exemplars of that heavenly foundation. All this enlarges the significance of Pope Paul's decision to re-emphasize this tradition of joint witness by abolishing the later, individual feast day of Paul and restoring the full significance of their joint festivity on June 29. And it supports a significant distinction of great ecumenical import: viz., St. Peter's primacy has always been that of *principatus,* St. Paul's that of *doctor.*

Professor Farmer and Fr. Kereszty leave their conclusions tentative and appropriately open-ended. But these conclusions are freighted with allowable inferences that invite their readers to further reflections, historical and otherwise. For example, what was the aboriginal nature of Christian unity in the early ages? In what sense was this unity what we now speak of as "organic"? Again, what does this shared witness of Peter and Paul have to tell us about the breadth and the limits of diversity within an authentic unity in Christ, and *koinonia* amongst "separated brothers and sisters" who nonetheless confess Jesus Christ in good faith as "Lord and Savior to the glory of God the Father"?

Ecumenical veterans are accustomed to the conventional distinctions between spiritual unity (. . . "we are one in the Spirit, we are one in the Lord . . ."), conciliar or confederated unity (as in the worldwide federations, alliances or families of churches—Lutheran, Presbyterian, Anglican—and also in the World Council of Churches, national Councils, united or uniting national churches, etc.) and organic union (i.e., fully mingled memberships, ministries and sacraments). We know well what great blessings have come to the Christian world from all the marvelous signs and wonders of spiritual unity (i.e., Christians in mutual recognition and fellowship), over the course of the last eight decades. But we also know how far the denominations still stand from each other in meaningful sacramental bondings. We appreciate the contributions to Christian peace and amity that have come from great conciliar events and from the ongoing conciliar process. But to what end? Can there be any truly complete unity other than that of a visible *koinonia* in Christ, as Head of a living Body? Is this not the basic reference for the metaphor "organic"? But if so, is it not tragically ironic that most of the proposed models for organic unity have actually been so obviously *in*organic—having more to do with juridical questions about hierarchical order, theoretical questions about doctrinal purity, practical questions about homologous structures than with vital integrity in the still living Body of Christ. Need one wonder, then, why the ecumenical movement, as we have known it in my lifetime, seems now so near to stalling speed? Is it possible that the church of the first Christian millenium (with its manifold turmoils and divisions) knew something about *organic* unity that then fell out of Christian memory and understanding in the tragic separations of the second millenium (with its more rigid norms of entire conformity?).

Professor Farmer and Fr. Kereszty have, in my view, succeeded in showing that the unity between Sts. Peter and Paul was truly *organic,* in the crucial sense that they acknowledged each other as "members one of another" in "the Body of Christ," despite deep-running differences of the sort that are natural in a living body (in both its forms and functions). They shared the same faith; they were accorded equivalent apostolic status in the early church; their leadership roles and martyrdoms in and for the church in Rome were linked. Their charisms were different, but "from the Self-Same Spirit." The New Testament witness (as in Galatians 2, Acts 15 and II Peter 2) allows for a very real Petrine primacy, which seems also to have been *inter pares.* It also points to wider limits of diversity than those now allowed in the dominant ecumenical models. This suggests, in turn, that if the "Peter-Paul Syndrome," described here by Professor Farmer and Fr. Kereszty could be taken up afresh as a paradigm, then new ecumenical horizons would open up, with new prospects for ecumenical convergences in place of the older patterns that prescribe some sort of "return" to some ecclesiological *status quo ante.* And for those of us who have been witnesses to so many ecumenical epiphanies in the epoch between Edinburgh (1910) and the Second Vatican Council (1962–65), and who have believed that they were authentic gifts of the Holy Spirit, such a scholarly restoration of the primal image of organic unity between Sts. Peter and Paul would be enough to rekindle our flagging hopes.

As we now see, the disagreements between the premier apostles, so frankly reported in Holy Writ, were serious enough to have stymied any ecumenical dialogue in which any of us have ever been engaged. Their concordance in the Council of Jerusalem fell short of anything now required by the definitions of organic unity in our latter-day models of it. But if we were as content with the authority of Sts. Peter *and* Paul, as Pope Nicholas was, there might arise new possibilities of some contemporary equivalent to their right hands in fellowship, new definitions of *organic* unity that still would be faithful to the apostolic originals.

It goes without saying, I hope, that these musings of mine are not strictly linear inferences from any of the arguments or conclusions of Professor Farmer and Fr. Kereszty. Other inferences are open. Some of them are positive (e.g., the still open question concerning the nature of episcopal collegiality, now in exciting debate and evolution in Roman Catholicism and, in quite different ambiances, among Protestants as well). Some possible conclusions could be negative (e.g., that the author of Acts and St. Irenaeus, between them, have glossed over differences that were not actually reconciled). But even this would help to underscore my main point: viz., that this is the sort of historical inquiry that is a resource of great import in the ongoing ecumenical dialogue.

Historical narrative is never simply extrapolative. Good history does not lend itself to confident prediction. But good history also stirs the imagination beyond old stereotypes. Thus, church history, in the spirit and style of this essay, can aid the development of a distinctive perspective and methodology that is critical, yet also ecumenical, in almost the root-meaning of *oikoumene* (i.e., "the civilized world," characterized by a shared universe of irenic discourse, integrated by a central loyalty, within wide limits of cultural diversity). One can hardly recall or imagine an age in which such a perspective was more needful for Christians who understand that they are living in a global circumstance in which *unity*-in-diversity is a prerequisite for survival, when unity-in-*diversity* is our only viable option.

Professor Farmer and Fr. Kereszty have thus served us well, with their insights and the measured care of their exposition of them. May their tribe increase, together with more *Christifideles* who are prepared to be edified and energized by the recovery of such "forgotten" resources from our apostolic heritage, for use in our ecumenical future.

Albert C. Outler

NOTES

[1]Cf. for example, *Peter in the New Testament,* ed. by R.E. Brown, K.P. Donfried and J. Reumann (Minneapolis: Augsburg Publishing H. and Paulist Press, 1973); "Lutherans and Catholics in Dialogue," in *Papal Primacy and the Universal Church,* ed. by P.C. Empie and T.A. Murphy (Minneapolis: Augsburg Publishing H., 1974); *A Pope for All Christians? An Inquiry into the Role of Peter in the Modern Church,* ed. by P.J. McCord (New York: Paulist Press, 1976); J.M. Miller, *What Are They Saying About Papal Primacy?* (New York: Paulist Press, 1983).

[2]European scholarship has rediscovered the importance of the joint Petrine-Pauline roots of the church of Rome long ago, while in America, up to the English translation of J.M.R. Tillard, *L'Evêque de Rome* (Paris: Cerf, 1982; ET: *The Bishop of Rome,* Wilmington, DE: Glazier, 1983) their findings remained relatively unknown. According to our knowledge, Tillard's book contains the best overall treatment of our theme from both an historical and a systematic viewpoint. Some important publications before this book are as follows: Y.M.J. Congar, "Saint Paul et l'autorité de l'église romaine d'après la Tradition," *Studiorum Paulinorum Congressus Internationalis Catholicus 1961, coll. Analecta Biblica,* 17–18, pp. 491–516. This is a detailed historical survey with theological conclusions. E. Lanne's "L'Eglise de Rome a gloriosissimis duobus apostolis Petro et Paulo Romae fundatae et constitutae ecclesiae (Adv Haer III, 3,2)," *Irénikon,* 49 (1976), pp. 275–322, is a detailed and nuanced investigation of our theme in the theological writings of the second century. An important Protestant publication is J.J. von Allmen, *La primauté de l'église de Pierre et de Paul* (Fribourg-Paris: Editions universitaires—Cerf, 1977). He shows the ecumenical significance of the historical and theological fact that the church of Rome is the church of both Peter and Paul.

[3]In this section we are heavily indebted to the works of Lanne, Tillard and Congar as quoted in note 2.

CHAPTER 2

¹J.B. Lightfoot, *The Apostolic Fathers,* Part I, S. Clement of Rome, Vol. II, p. 27, and Part II, S. Ignatius, S. Polycarp, Vol. II, Sec. 2, p. 922.

²See Birger Gerhardsson, *The Origins of the Gospel Traditions* (Fortress Press, 1978).

³In other contexts this verb means: "give an account of what one has learned," "record." As *historia* it is used in the sense of "inquiry"; it is so used in the title of a work by Theophrastus: "systematic (or scientific) observation." In the absolute it is used of "science," generally of "geometry," and in empirical medicine for "body of recorded cases." *Historia* is also used in the sense of "knowledge obtained through inquiry and observation," i.e. "information." And finally we have the meaning of *historia* as a "written account of one's inquiries," "narrative," and "history." See *A Greek-English Lexicon,* compiled by Henry George Liddell and Robert Scott, revised and augmented by Henry Stuart Jones (Oxford, 9th ed., 1940), Vol. I, p. 842. WZNT cites examples from Hellenistic Greek which mean simply "get to know," which meaning has been accepted by the translators of the NEB. However, on the basis of context, "visit a person for the purpose of inquiry" is to be preferred.

⁴"Galatians 1:18 ΙΣΤΟΡΣΑΙ ΚΗΦΑΝ," in *New Testament Essays: Studies in Memory of Thomas Walter Manson,* edited by A.J.B. Higgins (Manchester University Press, 1959), pp. 144–9.

⁵*Op. cit.* p. 149.

⁶*Op. cit.* p. 146.

⁷*Moralia* 516 C, and *De Curiositate* 2 (iii, 314 in the last Teubner edition).

⁸*A Critical and Exegetical Commentary on the Epistle to the Galatians* (Edinburgh: T. and T. Clark, 1921), p. 60.

⁹Baruch Sapir and Dov-Neeman, *Capernaum, History and Legacy, Art and Architecture* (Tel-Aviv, 1976,) p. 11.

¹⁰*Loc. cit.*

¹¹Other reasons supportive of the view that the evangelist Matthew wrote for readers who lived in Christian communities which were the fruit of early missionary activity from northern Galilee into southern Syria are given in "Some Thoughts on the Provenance of Matthew" by William R. Farmer, in *The Teacher's Yoke: Studies in Memory of Henry Trantham,* ed. E. Jerry Vardaman, and James Leo Garrett, Jr. (Waco: Baylor University Press, 1964), pp. 109–116.

¹²William R. Farmer, "Peter and Paul: A Constitutive Relationship for Catholic Christianity," *Texts and Testaments: Critical Essays on the Bible and Early Church Fathers,* a volume in honor of Stewart Dickson

Currie, ed. W. Eugene March (San Antonio: Trinity University Press, 1980), pp. 219–236, and "Peter and Paul," *Jesus and the Gospel, Tradition, Scripture, and Canon* (Philadelphia: Fortress Press, 1983), pp. 50–63.

[13]William R. Farmer and Denis Farkasfalvy, *The Formation of the New Testament Canon* (New York: Paulist Press, 1983), pp. 7–95.

[14]For the relationship of the apostolic norm of the "truth of the gospel" and the second century forms of the "regula," see William R. Farmer, "Galatians and the Second-Century Development of the 'Regula Fidei,'" *The Second Century* 4,3 (Fall 1984), pp. 143–70.

[15]*Marc* 4.2.1–5.

CHAPTER 3

[1]See 1 Clem 5.4–7; Ign. *Rom* 4.3; Eusebius, *Eccl Hist* 2.25.8.

[2]Cf. E. Lanne, *op. cit.* 301–306, 312–314.

[3]That one exception is *Ag Her* 1.13.16. For an explanation of the reversed order, see E. Lanne, *op. cit.* 295.

[4]*Ibid.* 300.

[5]This passage also reveals that the Valentinians themselves held the teaching of both Peter and Paul in high esteem.

[6]The words in brackets are missing in the Latin text and were reconstructed in the French critical edition: Irenaeus of Lyons, *Contre les hérésies*, Livre III, edited by A. Rousseau and L. Doutreleau (*Sources Chrétiennes* vol. 210; Paris: Cerf 1974), pp. 304–305. Subsequently, this edition will be referred to as *SC*.

[7]Paul's letters did indeed serve in the hands of the gnostics as a powerful starting point for their speculations. See E.H. Pagels, *The Gnostic Paul. Gnostic Exegesis of the Pauline Letters* (Philadelphia: Fortress, 1975).

[8]My translation is a modified version of the *Early Christian Fathers,* translated and edited by C.C. Richardson (The Library of Christian Classics, vol. 1) (Philadelphia: Westminster Press, 1953), p. 370.

[9]See W.R. Farmer and D.M. Farkasfalvy, *The Formation of the New Testament Canon. An Ecumenical Approach* (New York: Paulist, 1983), pp. 71–73.

[10]I modified the translation of *Early Christian Fathers,* p. 372 according to the reconstructed Greek text of *SC* vol. 211, p. 33.

[11]See *SC,* vol. 210, pp. 233–236 and E. Lanne, *op. cit.* 275–322. The latest evaluation of literature on the exegesis of *Ag Her* 3.3.2 appeared in M.A. Donovan, "Irenaeus in Recent Scholarship," *The Second Cen-*

tury 4 (1984) 238–240. I will mention here only two less recent but influential interpretations that diverge from mine. Ludwig sees in *principalitas* the abstract form of the noun *princeps,* in Greek *koryphaios,* the most widespread title for the apostle Peter among the Greek Fathers. Consequently, the translation of the phrase would be: "because of its more excellent leadership position." This would point, with some probability, to Matthew 16:18–19 where Peter receives his leadership position from Jesus. In this case Paul would be mentioned in Irenaeus' text merely "out of an old habit," as "part of a formula," not because Irenaeus considers Paul's church-founding activity in Rome constitutive for the *principalitas* of that church with regard to all other churches. See *op. cit.* p. 9. Batiffol translates *principalitas* as *prōteia* meaning "firstness"; C.P. Batiffol, *Cathedra Petri. Étude d'histoire ancienne de l'Église* (Paris: Cerf, 1938), pp. 35–37. *The Patristic Greek Lexicon,* under the word *prōteia,* also accepts this interpretation. Batiffol thinks that Irenaeus uses the term here in the same sense as Cyprian will in the third century. Rome would be the first among all the churches not because she was founded first but because she was founded by the first of the apostles, Peter. Peter received the apostolic commission from Christ first before all the other apostles as Matthew 16:19 attests. Therefore he is the model, the prototype of apostleship, and so is the church of Rome that participates in the office of Peter. According to Batiffol, then, *principalitas* refers to Matthew 16:17–19, but in a different sense from what Ludwig supposed. Batiffol, too, ignores the role of Paul for the church of Rome. See *op. cit.* pp. 35–37. However, Ludwig's interpretation lacks any textual support in Irenaeus. The phrase *koryphaios tōn apostolōn* does not occur in any second century text and appears to be a much later creation. Batiffol's hypothesis cannot be ruled out, but one cannot prove it from any text in *Ag Her.*

¹²*Ag Her* 1.26.1; 31.1; 4.35.2.

¹³3.2.8; 17.2.

¹⁴2.13.1; 17.3; 4.26.2; 5.14.1–2; 21.1.

¹⁵3.15.3; 16.6; 4.20.2; 38.3.

¹⁶See *SC,* vol. 210, p. 243.

¹⁷For establishing the probability of the adjective *hikanoteran,* see *SC,* vol. 210, p. 232.

¹⁸*Quibus* (to the barbarian tribes who cannot read the scriptures yet adhere to the original tradition of the apostles) *si aliquis adnuntiaverit ea quae ab hereticis adinventa sunt . . . statim concludentes aures longo longius fugient. . . . Sic per illam veterum apostolorum traditionem ne in conceptionem quidem mentis admittunt quodcumque horum porten-*

tiloquium est ET (3.4.2). Cf. also the way Irenaeus compares the apostles and the heretics: *apostoli, cum sint his omnibus vetustiores* (3.21.3).

[19]*Ante Valentinum enim non fuerunt qui sunt a Valentino, neque ante Marcionem erant qui sunt a Marcione. . . . . Reliqui vero qui vocantur Gnostici, a Menandro Simonis discipulo, quemadmodum ostendimus, accipientes initia (tas archas), unusquisque eorum cuius participatus est sententiae, eius et pater et antistes apparuit. Omnes autem hi multo posterius, mediantibus iam ecclesiae temporibus, insurrexerunt in suam apostasiam* (3.4.3).

[20]*Quapropter eis qui in ecclesia sunt presbyteris obaudire oportet, his qui successionem habent ab apostolis, sicut ostendimus, qui cum episcopatus successione charisma veritatis.certum secundum placitum Patris acceperunt, reliquos vero qui absistunt a principali successione et quocumque loco colligunt suspectos habere* (4.26.2).

[21]"Whenever a controversy arises, even if it is about a small matter, *nonne oporteret in antiquissimas recurrere ecclesias in quibus apostoli conversati sunt et ab eis de praesenti quaestione sumere quod certum et vere liquidum est?*" (3.4.1).

[22]Cf. Rom 1.8.

[23]See note 11.

[24]Cf. E. Lanne, *op. cit.* p. 297.

[25]For points 1 through 4 see E. Lanne, *op. cit.* pp. 286–94. Cf. also H.F. von Campenhausen, *Die Idee des Martyriums in der alten Kirche,* 2nd ed. (Göttingen: Vandenhoeck and Ruprecht, 1964), esp. p. 48.

[26]E. Lanne, *op. cit.* 294–301.

[27]For the details of the paschal controversy, see V. Loi, "Controversia pasquale," *Dizionario Patristico e di Antichit Cristiane,* ed. A. Di Berardino (Casale Monferrator: Marieti, 1983) vol. 2, cols. 2695–97; C. Mohrmann, "Le conflit pascale au IIe siècle," *VChr* 16 (1962) 154–71; T. J. Talley, *The Origins of the Liturgical Year* (New York: Pueblo, 1986), pp. 13–30.

[28]Cf. E. Lanne, *op. cit.* p. 307.

[29]Victor may have never carried out the threat of excommunication or his successors may have disregarded it, for Eusebius testifies that the Quartodeciman practice survived up to the Council of Nicea and those who observed it were not considered heretics. The council legislated uniformity in this matter. See Eusebius, *Life of Constantine* 3.14–24; cf. also Socrates, *Ecclesiastical History* 1.8–9.

[30]In Tertullian's lapidary style: *Petri cohibentis eodem ore quia eodem et spiritu, quo Paulus* (*Prayer* 20.2). I quote the words of Tertullian

according to the critical edition: Q.S.F. Tertulliani *Opera,* vols I & II (Corpus Christianorum. Series Latina vols. I & II) (Brepols: Turnholti, 1954).

[31]While admitting that Peter may have committed a fault, Tertullian excuses him even in *Pre* by referring to 1 Corinthians 9:19–21. He points out that Paul himself practiced at another time what he reprehended in Peter (23.10).

[32]Cf. also another text according to which Paul goes up to Jerusalem *ad cognoscendos apostolos et consultandos ne non secundum illos credidisset et non secundum illos evangelizaret (Marc* 4.2.5). Note also that Tertullian changes the order of the three pillars from James, Cephas and John as found in Galatians 2:9, to Peter, John, and James, the order of Luke 9:28 in the transfiguration scene (*Marc* 4.3.3; 5.3.6).

[33]Tertullian is the first, to my knowledge, to mention the Roman sojourn and confession of faith of John. The next one to mention it is Jerome who explicitly refers to Tertullian (*Com on Matt* 20.23; *Ag Jov* 1.26). Cf. the notes of the French critical edition: Tertullien, *Traité de la préscription contre les hérétiques,* ed. R.F. Refoulé (*SC,* vol. 46, Paris: Cerf, 1957), p. 138.

[34]Even the Montanist Tertullian acknowledges the decisive influence of Rome over the universal church. He reproaches Praxeas for pressuring the bishop of Rome to change his mind about the Montanist movement. Tertullian is convinced that if the bishop of Rome had accepted the "new prophecy" (Montanism), by that acceptance he would have conferred peace on the churches of Asia and Phrygia: *ex ea agnitione pacem ecclesiis Asiae et Phrygiae inferentem.* In other words, then, all the bishops of Asia and Phrygia would have made peace with it (*Prax* 1.5). Cf. Batiffol, *op. cit.* p. 34.

[35]See the development of this belief below, pp. 89–95.

[36]See Ludwig, *op. cit.* p. 11.

[37]Note that *monogamous* here means: one who married only once.

[38]H. F. von Campenhausen, *Kirchliches Amt und geistliche Vollmacht in den ersten drei Jahrhunderten* (Tübingen, 1953), p. 222.

[39]See P. Batiffol, *Cathedra Petri,* pp. 95–195; A. Demoustier, "Episcopat et union à Rome selon saint Cyprien," *Rech Sc Rel* (July-September 1964) 337–69.

[40]The Montanist Tertullian denounces the Catholic church for extending the power of forgiving capital sins to the martyrs. He mocks the custom that as soon as someone takes up some light chains, he is surrounded by fornicators whose tears make pools around him (*Mod* 22.1). Other public sinners run to the mines from where they return as *com-*

municatores. They are again in communion with the church and allowed to receive sacramental communion (*ibid.* 22.2).

[41]B. Poschmann, *Penance and the Anointing of the Sick* (New York: Herder and Herder, 1964), p. 77. The letter says about the martyrs that "they loosed everyone and did not bind anyone" (Eus., *Eccl Hist* 5.2.5).

[42]Dionysius reports to Fabius of Antioch:

> The divine martyrs among us who now sit by Christ's side as partners in his kingdom, share his authority, and are his fellow-judges, opened their arms to their fallen brethren who faced the charge of sacrificing. Seeing their conversion and repentance, they were sure that it would be acceptable to him who does not in the least desire the death of a sinner, but rather his repentance; so they received them, admitted them to the congregation and allowed them to take part in services and feasts. What, then, brothers, is your advice to us in this matter? What must we do? Shall we take our stand in full agreement with them, uphold their merciful decision, and deal gently with those they pitied? Or shall we condemn their decision as improper, and set ourselves up as judges of their attitude, wound their gentleness, and turn their practice upside down? (*Eccl. Hist.* 5.42.5, translated and introduced by G.A. Williamson, New York: Penguin Books, 1981, pp. 279–280).

What theological convictions justified such participation of the martyrs in the reconciliation of penitents? Since the martyr (and even "the martyr designate," later called "confessor") is most perfectly conformed to Christ in his suffering, the Holy Spirit dwells in him and thus his prayer is one with the prayer of Christ and of the Holy Spirit. When he prays, the Holy Spirit prays in him and therefore his prayer is most effective in obtaining pardon for sins. His suffering, through the communion of saints, may help the purification of the sinner and thus reduce or eliminate the need for ecclesiastical penance. Moreover, the martyr, under the inspiration of the Holy Spirit, is able to discern the inner state of the penitent, whether or not he is sufficiently contrite and spiritually healed so that he is ready for reconciliation with God. At that time the role of the bishop and of the church was seen in similar terms to that of the martyrs: the local church under the leadership of the bishop interceded for the penitent and the bishop decided when the penitent was ripe for reconciliation. When the time came, the bishop solemnly readmitted the penitent into the church knowing that communion with the church obtains communion with God. In this complex process the specific role of the bishop was not always clearly perceived. At any rate, from the tenor of bishop Dionysius' letter it appears that he considers himself the final arbiter and agent of readmitting the penitent into the church. Although somewhat unsure, he leans toward abiding by the martyr's decision.

Cyprian, after the Decian persecution, did not allow the martyrs to readmit the apostates to the peace of the church. Yet he also took into account their intercession in reducing the time of public penance. Cf. *Epist* 20–6.

⁴³The goal of the Montanist Tertullian in *On Modesty* is to attack the validity and show the absurdity of what he calls an "edict." This "edict" probably issued by the Catholic bishop of Carthage, Agrippinus, defends the church's practice of forgiving fornicators after they have done public penance. In order to prove his point, Tertullian makes several assertions that do not seem consistent with one another. On the one hand, he claims that the "peccata capitalia" (sometimes only three—murder, fornication and apostasy—sometimes more than these three) could be forgiven by God's power that has been given as a personal privilege to a prophet or to an apostle. According to Matthew 16:18–19 Peter received this power as a personal non-transmittable privilege (21.5–10). On the other hand, a few lines later Tertullian declares that "no power of loosing and binding for the capital sins of the faithful has been conferred on Peter." Besides the key of doctrine and forgiving sins through baptism, the power of the keys and that of loosing and binding mean only the commission to make disciplinary decisions and to forgive the sins of a brother against a brother in the church (21.11–15).

⁴⁴Most experts agree that the phrase "ecclesia Petri propinqua" is the abbreviated form of "ecclesia ecclesiae Petri propinqua."

⁴⁵See *On Monogamy* 8.4. Note that in *On Modesty* 21.9.10 (understood in the light of *Antidote* 10.8) the claim of the Catholic bishop that Tertullian quotes and refutes is not based directly on apostolic succession but on a particular interpretation of Matthew 16 as explained on pp. 77–80.

⁴⁶For instance, Ludwig, *op. cit.,* states: "Wir möchten jedoch, besonders im Hinblick auf die spätere Exegese, noch einmal ausdrücklich wiederholen, dass hier, wo die altkirchliche Literatur überhaupt zum erstenmal Mt 16:18–19 deutet, petra auf den Apostel Petrus, nicht aber auf Christus oder den Glauben bezogen wird." Ludwig omits the important point that Jesus gives one of his own "figures" to Peter (*Marc* 4.13.6).

[47]In later fathers there is also a third line of interpretation: the faith of Peter is the rock on which the church is built. Cf. Origen, *Cat Fragm* 345.11. To illustrate the variety of interpretations among the fathers, I quote from the response of E. Ferguson to my paper (from which I developed the present chapter): "Augustine in a famous passage in the *Retractions* (1.21) says he had formerly understood the rock as Peter, which seems to have been standard North African interpretation, but had come to understand it as Christ, and he leaves it to the reader to decide which of the two interpretations is the more probable." Other interpreters seemingly did not feel it was necessary to make a choice. Hilary of Poitiers in the same work, *On the Trinity,* could understand the rock as Peter (6.20), as the confession made by Peter (2.23;6.36), and as faith itself (6.37). Jerome gives more choices: Peter (*Comm on Mt* 16:18), the chair of Peter (*Ep* 15.2), all of the apostles along with Peter (*Ag Jov* 1.26), and Christ (*ibid.,* 2.37). Ambrose is similarly varied: Peter (*Faith* 4.5.57), faith (*Expos in Lk* 6.97–8), and Christ (*Ep* 43.9: "founded by the teaching of Peter on the rock Christ"). John Chrysostom was singularly single-minded; for him the church is consistently stated to have been built on the faith confessed by Peter (*Hom on Mt* 54.3; 82.3; *Comm on Gal* 1:1). These three lines of interpretation fit together into a synthesis if we accept Origen's explanation: Jesus is the true rock of the church but Peter also becomes rock by participating in Jesus through faith (cf. *Hom in Exod* 5.4; *Comm on Mt* 12.11–14).

CHAPTER 4

[1]Strangely enough, this joint foundation is asserted by those fathers who must have known from the letter to the Romans and from the Acts of the Apostles that Paul did not historically "found" the church of Rome. In the light of today's historical evidence this joint "founding" must be interpreted as a theological assertion with some historical foundation rather than a strictly historical statement describing a merely historical process. The Christian community in Rome did already exist before Paul, and most probably before Peter came to that city. They "founded" the church of Rome by making it the depository of their apostolic teaching and by confirming their teaching with their martyrdom. In the words of Tertullian, the apostles "poured their whole teaching along with their blood" into the church of Rome (*Pre* 36, 3).

[2] ... *In quibus* [*partibus*] *apostoli quotidie sedent et cruor ipsorum sine intermissione Dei gloriam testatur;* quoted by Congar, "Saint Paul et l'autorité de l'église romaine d'après la Tradition," 496.

[3] *Sermon 82, On the Feastday of Peter and Paul,* n. 1.

[4] *Ibid,* n. 7.

[5] H. Denzinger & A. Schönmetzer, *Enchiridion Symbolorum* (Freiburg im Br.: Herder, 1965) 26th ed., p. 350. From now on quoted as *DS.* The exact date of the document is uncertain, probably the second half of the fifth or beginning of the sixth century.

[6] Cf. Y.M.J. Congar, "S. Nicolas I (+867): ses positions ecclésiologiques" *Rivista di Storia della Chiesa in Italia* 21 (1967) 396. According to Congar, in initiating this practice, Nicholas goes back to the Gelasian Decree. By associating the authority of Paul with that of Peter, Nicholas indicates all that the universal church has for the church of Rome: *Suscepit ergo ac continet in se Romana ecclesia, quod Deus universalem ecclesiam suscipere ac continere praecepit.*

[7] *Epist.* 86 quoted by Congar, "Saint Paul et l'autorité de l'église romaine d'après la Tradition," 502.

[8] Cf. *ibid.* 503.

[9] *DS* 2803, 3903. Cf. Tillard, *op. cit.* 79–80.

[10] "Homily of Pope Paul VI on the Feast of Saints Peter and Paul, June 29, 1977," *The Pope Speaks* 22 (1977) 309.

[11] This seems to me to be the focal point of the twofold dogmatic definition at Vatican I concerning the infallibility which the pope possesses, under some well-defined conditions, and concerning his supreme immediate and universal jurisdiction. Cf. *DS* 3050–3075.

[12] Cf. Tillard, *op. cit.* p. 93, n. 90.

[13] Congar quotes several texts from the tradition of the church, texts which explain why Paul is often pictured as sitting on the right side of Jesus. He is superior to Peter because he was called by the glorified Christ while Peter was appointed by the earthly Christ. See *op. cit.* p. 495.

[14] Peter Damian's work *De picturis principum apostolorum* is a most impressive treatise on explaining all the reasons for a long Catholic tradition that, from a certain viewpoint, Paul is superior to Peter. The following are only the most important points not treated in our book. Peter symbolizes the active life, Paul the contemplative life. His love is so great as to embrace the whole world. He has founded the universal church since he has sown the seed of the faith everywhere. Thus, in a similar way to Christ, he presides not only over one church, but, "without injury to the right of the other apostles, he appears to preside over all the churches" (Migne, *PL* 145, 591–595).

[15] Cf. Congar, *op cit.* p. 500.

[16] These statements are true only in the sense of predominant characteristics. Peter is the first witness to the risen Christ and receives the task

of being the chief shepherd over the disciples from the risen Lord, and it is essential for Paul that the Son of God is a descendant of David according to the flesh.

[17]Again, historically, Peter and Paul cannot be identified exclusively as representatives, respectively, of institution versus that of charism. Peter's office is based on his gift of faith which he received from the revelation of the Father, and Paul is most emphatic in subordinating all charisms to his apostolic authority.

[18]Again, we must admit that this image of Paul as a missionary to the Gentiles is already corrected in the New Testament itself which presents Peter as the initiator of the first Gentile mission (Acts 10) and as author of two letters whose addressees are predominantly Gentile Christians or at least include Gentile Christians.

[19]The objects of the first such rejection were the Montanist charismatics in Phrygia. Cf. Tertullian, *Prax* 1.5.

[20]*Acta Apostolicae Sedis* 70 (1978) 394. This long tradition of joining the church of Rome to both Peter and Paul, a tradition which runs from Irenaeus to Pope Paul VI, is not contradicted by two decrees of the Holy See. The first in 1647 condemns a Jansenist opinion according to which the apostolic church had two equal heads, Peter and Paul. But the decree does not deny that Peter and Paul may be equal under some aspect other than juridical. See *DS* 1999. Pius X reiterates the same condemnation during the Modernist crisis. See *DS* 3555.

[21]Ignatius of Ant., *Letter to the Romans,* II, 1.

[22]See n. 2.

[23]See n. 2 and the statement of the presbyter Philip at Ephesus about eter "who has lived and judged in his successors up to now and always will." *Acta Conciliorum Oecumenicorum,* ed. E. Schwarts (Berlin & Leipzig: Walter de Gruyter & Co., 1927) I, 1, 3 p. 60.

[24]The ancient text is to be found in *Das frankische Sacramentarium Gelasianum in alemannischer Überlieferung (Codex Sangall No. 348)* 2nd ed., published by K. Mohlberg (Liturgiegeschichtliche Quellen 112; Münster in Westfalien, 1939), p. 148. It was adopted by the Missal of Pope Paul VI with some changes. There is only one change which affects its theology: *quos operis tui vicarios eidem contulisti praeesse pastores* is changed into *quos Filii tui vicarios eidem contulisti praeesse pastores (Missale Romanum,* Rome, 1970, p. 426). The change makes explicit the christological representation of the apostolate.

[25]*Quia tunc salvari posse confidimus, si eorum precibus tua gubernetur ecclesia, quibus utitur te constituente principibus.* Cf. also *ut eorum supplicationibus muniamur, quorum regimur principatu. Das frankische Sacramentarium Gelasianum,* pp. 149, 151.

[26]Cf. Y.M.J. Congar, "Die Apostolizität der Kirche" in *Mysterium Salutis 4/1 Das Heilsgeschehen in der Gemeinde* (Einsiedeln: Benziger, 1972), p. 539, and H. Urs von Balthasar, *The Office of Peter and the Structure of the Church,* p. 159.

[27]P. Brown documents this belief with numerous examples. He also shows why such belief cannot be explained as a somewhat modified form of pagan popular traditions. The pagan world of antiquity believed in a chasm between the realm of the dead bodies of mortal human beings and that of the immortal gods. The rising cult of the relics and tombs of the martyrs was met with a sarcasm and horror among pagan writers. Cf. P. Brown, *The Cult of the Saints* (Chicago: University of Chicago Press, 1981), pp. 1–22.

[28]Cf. *Antidote* 15, 3.

[29]Cf. M. Righetti, *Manuale di storia liturgica,* vol. 2 (Milan: Ancora, 1955), pp. 348–349.

[30]For instance, Gregory VII asked for their help against Henry IV, and Leo X against Luther. See Congar, "Saint Paul et l'autorité de l'église romaine d'après la Tradition," 505.

[31]*Adfuit palmae qui contentioni non defuit; iuvit animorum vota nostrorum qui videret symbolo (a) se primo inter apostolos tradito derogari Acta Conc. Oecumen.* I, 2, p. 107.

[32]See Congar, *op cit.* 505.

[33]*Byzantine Daily Worship* by J. Raya & J. de Vinck (Tournai, Belgium: Desclée & Cie., 1969).

[34]*DS* 181.

[35]*Acta Conc. Oec.* I, 2 p. 109.

[36]*Ibid.* I, 1, 3 p. 60.

[37]*Ibid.* p. 57.

[38]Probably the quote from the letter of the Synod of Arles which I chose as the motto of this article echoes Matthew 19:28. See J. Dupont's article, "Le logion des douze trônes," *Biblica* 45 [1962], pp. 355–92, which points out that the early church understood that the apostles continue to act through the bishops.

[39]Cf. the letter of Nicolaus I in which he explains the effect of what Peter and Paul have done for the church of Rome: *Sanctam Romanam Ecclesiam roseo cruore suo consecrarunt, et hanc non habentem maculam, aut rugam, aut aliquid hujusmodi exhibentes, Deo Domino dedicaverunt* (*Epist* 86, quoted by Congar, *op. cit.,* 502. Cf. also the *Decretum Gelasianum: Est ergo prima Petri Apostoli Sedis* [*sedes*] *Romanae Ecclesiae, non habens maculam neque rugam nec aliquid eiusmodi* (*DS* 351). I believe that more research would show that the same eschatological character could be attributed to the exercise of the teaching activity of

the whole episcopal college. Present in their teaching through the bishops, the apostles lead the church toward the eschatological consummation.

[40]Homily on the feast of Saints Peter and Paul in 1978 a few months before his death quoted in *AAS* 70 (1978).

[41]Orthodox theology has a deep understanding of this presence of the *eschata* in our world. According to J.D. Zizioulas, in the eschatological approach to apostolicity "l'apostolicité vient à l'Église *du côté du future*. C'est l'anticipation de la fin, la nature finale de l'Église qui révèlent son caractère apostolique. Ce serait se méprendre sur cette anticipation que de le concevoir comme psychologique; il ne s'agit pas du sentiment éprouvé dans l'expectative ou l'espérance de ce qui est offert par elle, mais d'une *présence* réelle *hic et nunc* des *eschata*. 'C'est maintenant le jugement du monde' (Jn 12:31), et c'est maintenant en ce moment simple du *nun* johannique—que l'histoire entière est consommée" ("La continuité avec les origines apostoliques dans la conscience théologique des églises orthodoxes," *Istina* 19 [1974], 71). Zizioulas, however, does not point out in his admirable synthesis on apostolicity that in the patristic tradition of both east and west the apostles (and, to a lesser extent, all the saints) are associated with this anticipated presence and judging activity of the glorified Christ in his church.

[42]Troparion in the Byzantine liturgy: *Byzantine Daily Worship*, p. 715.

CHAPTER 5

[1]See Sermon 82, "On the Feastday of Peter and Paul," mentioned on pp. 44–45 and in n. 3 of Chapter 4. There may be a basis in scripture for the experience of apostolic presence in the church.

[2]See Chapter 4, n. 1.

[3]See "The Apostolic Presence of Paul," in William R. Farmer and Denis M. Farkasfalvy, O. Cist., *The Formation of the New Testament Canon: An Ecumenical Approach* (Paulist Press, 1983), p. 54.

CHAPTER 6

[1]The Roman Catholic church has defined this dogma at Vatican I. Cf. *DS* 3050–3075.

[2]*Letter to Eulogius Alexandrinus* (*PL* 77, 933).

[3]Cf. *Lumen Gentium* 22 and the *Prefatory Note* to Chapter III of *LG*. Yet for the sake of full communion with other Christian churches, a pope, for the duration of his own pontificate, may announce to limit vol-

untarily such an exercise of authority. Cf. P. Granfield, *The Limits of the Papacy* (New York: Crossroad, 1985), pp. 178–193.

[4]One cannot exclude the possibility of invalid papal actions, for instance, trying to teach a doctrine opposed to God's revelation. In such case, obviously the critic should call attention to this fact also. We are unable to treat here the various levels and modes of criticism. The best treatment of the role of criticism in the service of the church's renewal from both an historical and a doctrinal point of view remains even today. Y.M. J. Congar, *Vraie et fausse réforme dans l'Église* (Paris: Cerf, 1950).

SUBJECT-NAME INDEX

academic colleagueship between Protestants and Roman Catholics, 99

Acts: author of, 136; first half dominated by Peter and second half by Paul, 7; in middle of canon reflecting composition of canon, 7; structure of, 7

Acts of the Apostles, 14, 146

adinventiones, heresies as human inventions, 59

Africa, missionary thrust to, 10, 88

agape, employed in exercising authority, 21

agreement and unanimity, right hand as sign of, 69

agreement of Peter and Paul: against Marcion and gnostics, 80; "handshake" in Jerusalem, 80; origin in common revelation, 80

Agrippinus: bishop of Carthage, 78; Catholic bishop of Carthage, 145

Allmen, J. J. von, 1, 138

Ambrose, 146

Ambrosiaster, Paul's visit an acknowledgement of "the primacy of Peter," 32

American Christianity, spectrum of, 132

American Society of Church History, award for ecumenical church history, 131

ancestry, common, 3

ancient tradition, reaffirmation by magisterium, 84

"and I remained with him," Paul's meaning (Gal 1:18), 28

"and I remained with him fifteen days" (Gal 1:18), 36–39

Anicetus, bishop of Rome, 67, 68

Annales of Baronius, 130

Antioch: Ignatius of, 4; martyrdom in, 106

Antioch on the Orontes, 105

Antiochene tradition of exegesis, possible source of Chrysostom's comment on *historesai,* 31

apostates, and Cyprian, 145

apostle, Ignatius not, 18

apostle to the Gentiles, authority for tradition concerning the Lord's supper, 26

apostle-bishops, 76

apostles: 5; appearances of the risen Lord to, 6; blood and teaching of, 71; founding by, 5; (Peter and Paul) "poured their whole teaching along with their blood" into the church of Rome (Tertullian, *Pre* 36.3), 99–100; present work of, 91; substitute or deputy shepherds, 91; succession from, 59; successors of, 57; two most glorious, 14; tradition coming from, 5; tradition of, 57; twelve, 54

Apostles' Creed, 99
apostleship, theological
    connection with martyrdom, 9
apostolic authority, charisms
    subordinated to, 88
apostolic authority, Paul's, 36
apostolic college, 124
apostolic commission,
    exhortation to martyrdom
    (Matt 10:16–22) in, 104
apostolic conference (Gal 2:1–10):
    Paul returns to Jerusalem after
    fourteen years for, 29;
    presupposed theological
    agreement of Peter and Paul
    tested by fourteen years of
    missionary work and
    constituted *magna charta* of
    holy catholic church, 47
apostolic faith: 99; "Catholic
    substance" of, 127; living word
    of God, 128–29; no deviation
    from, 126
apostolic faith of the church,
    articulation of, 126
apostolic gravesites, care for by
    bishop of Rome, 113
apostolic heritage: church of
    Rome, 127; "forgotten"
    resources from, 137
apostolic independence, Paul's, 36
apostolic institutions, 126
apostolic literature, 3
apostolic martyrdom of Peter and
    Paul. *See* martyrdom, apostolic
apostolic ministry, martyrdom
    essential to, 90
apostolic mission: 5; martyrdom
    constitutive of, 82, 89
apostolic power of Paul, 24
apostolic presence, Paul's in
    Corinth, 25
apostolic succession: 145;
    distinguished from juridical
    model, 91–92

apostolic way of life, no deviation
    from, 126
apostolic witness, 3, 4
apostolic witness in New
    Testament, rests on mutual
    trust between Peter and Paul,
    33
apostolic writings, public reading
    of, 73
appearances, resurrection. *See*
    resurrection appearances
Arabia, Paul's initial destination
    after conversion, 29
arche/archaion, origin/original,
    ancient, 59
argument in Galatians, to
    establish that Paul was not
    dependent for his authority to
    preach the gospel upon those
    who had been apostles before
    him, 36
Aristippus, 32
Arles, synod of, 4
Asia: missionary thrust to, 10, 88;
    Polycarp in, 17
Asia Minor: Irenaeus from, 14;
    Irenaeus with strong ties to, 13
atoning sacrifice, Jesus Christ,
    119
atoning power of the gospel, 13
*auctoritate Apostolorum Petri et
    Pauli,* introduction of Roman
    acts by, 84
Augustine: 76, 80, 146; Paul's
    visit a token of friendship, 32;
    Peter first apostle or bishop of
    Rome, 81
authentia, sovereignty, 59
authority of Rome, gradual
    transformation, 125

Babylon: church which dwells in,
    17; code name, 112; designates
    Rome as power hostile to God,
    8; 1 Peter from, 8; where King

Nebuchadnezzar persecuted the faithful of Jerusalem, 15
Balthasar, H. Urs von, 149
baptism, administration of, 76
Barnabas, 6
Batiffol, C. P.: 141, 143; traditional Catholic exegesis (Irenaeus, *Ag. Her.* 3.3.2), 61
"Be ye imitators of me," including faithful obedience unto death, 25
"Be ye imitators of me, as I am of Christ" (1 Cor 11:1), 26
Berardino, A. Di, 142
Bernard of Clairvaux, charges by, 127–28
Bernini Colonnade, in Piazza San Pietro, 133
Bethsaida, 39
bishop: final arbiter of public penance, 77; power of loosing and binding, 79
bishop of church in Rhone Valley, 114–15
bishop of Rome: 5, 11; action in a local church, 128; addresses church in Corinth from Paul's first Corinthian letter, 23; as final arbiter, 126; authority, 126; authority in calling on the authority of Paul, 24; authority of Peter and Paul, 82–83; charism of, 127; charism to teach faith of church with authority, 11; collegial acts, 126; collegial authority, 2, 124; exclusion of churches from Asia Minor, 114; guardian and harmonizer of Christian tradition, 88; "heir no less to Paul than to Peter," 118; heir of martyr apostles, 123; heir of Paul and Peter, 123; heir to Peter, 85–86; heritage of Peter and Paul, 118; jurisdiction of,

113; local, 115; meeting with, 114; ministry of universal service, 124; missionary to Gentiles, 88; "no less an heir to Paul than to Peter," 11; official documents of, 1; open to charisms of Spirit, 88; Peter as first only in third century, 4; Peter not first, 4; Petrine heritage, 117; power to exclude, 113; presence of Peter, 93; present, 116; previous, 115; primacy, 2, 123, 127; primacy and infallibility as successor of Peter, 96; pressure from Praxeas, 143; relationship to Peter and Paul, 11, 123; rest of episcopacy, 125; right and obligation to intervene with authority in the life of another local church, 11; role of, 11; servant of the Lord, 118; shepherding and teaching of, 96; successor of Peter, 2, 83, 85; threatened act of, 115; united witness of New Testament, 87; vicar (or successor) of Peter, 85; "vicar of Peter" in Pauline terms, 88; vicar or successor of Peter, 107; with heads of other churches, 117–18; witness to Jesus of Nazareth and risen Lord, 87
bishops: ministry of college of apostles, 96; Roman Catholic, 107; succession of, 58
bishops and deacons, church orders, 76
bishops of Asia and Phrygia, peace with montanism, 143
bishops of Asia Minor, Easter controversy, 67
bishops of Palestine, Pontus, Gaul, and Osroenes, synod 67

bishops of Rome: 1, 4; refer in patristic age to Peter's carrying on his ministry through them but describe the ministry by the Pauline "sollicitudo omnium ecclesiarum" (2 Cor 11:28), 4
blood of Christians, seed, 72
Brown, R. E., 138
Brown, P., 149
burial sites, custodian of, 105
Burton, Ernest DeWitt, 36
"by the way of the sea," Capernaum, 42
Byzantine church, prayers of Peter and Paul, 93
Byzantine liturgy, cult of apostles, 97

canon: 9–10; Acts in middle reflecting composition, 7; composition of, 6; development of New Testament, 4; formation of New Testament, 6; implicit, 10; martyr's, 13; New Testament, 3; scripture, 3; second half dominated by Pauline corpus, 7; structure of, 6
canon of scriptures, 13
Campenhausen, H. F. von, 76, 142–43
Capernaum: 40; Christians here would have been first to appreciate Matthean hermeneutical development of Isaiah 9:1–2, 44; prominent position at crossroads of land and sea routes north and east from Galilee, 41; suitable base for mission into southern Syria, 44
capital of Roman empire, 105
Catherine of Siena, charges by, 127
Catholic, 98

Catholic church: 98; shared leadership in, 133: See Roman Catholic church
Catholic church in Carthage, faith of, 77
"Catholic substance," apostolic faith, 127
Catholics, 10
center of unity: grave markers of martyred apostles, 112; Peter from Vatican I, 85
central loyalty, discourse integrated by, 136
century: fourth, 4; third, 4
"Cephas party," 49
charism: bishop of Rome, 127; Paul's vocation as, 87
charismatic movements, popes allied with, 88
Chorazin, 39
Christ: appearance to Paul, 34; atoning death and resurrection of, 6; bodily suffering of, 16; commission from, 141; conformed to, 144; gospel of the crucified and risen, 24; his blood is the price of freedom, 18; his sacrificial death as chief model for the faithful, 15; his suffering linked with suffering of the faithful, 16; institution of, 76; new life in, 5; prayer of, 144; present *kyrios* and king, 90; revealing activity in Irenaeus, 55; suffering, 24; suffering and reign by apostles, 90; teachings of, 5; *the* Rock, 134; witness to, 86; witnessing to, 5
Christian, as martyr, 16
Christian community (in Rome): 13, 99, 105, 112; and subsequent church of Rome, 105; before Paul and Peter, 146; its ontic shock from the

martyrdoms of Peter and Paul, 102

Christian faith, 34

Christian mystery, reintegrating of the dogma into totality of, 3

Christian origins, understanding of dependence upon mutual trust between Peter and Paul, 33

Christian unity: aboriginal nature of, 134; aided by historical understanding, 131; implications for, 131

Christ-like examples, martyred apostles Peter and Paul, 15

Christians: facing persecution, 16; Roman, 7

Christians from Asia Minor, residing in Rome, 114

Christians living in Rome, Paul's supervisional care for, 101

Christ's suffering, Christian martyr's opportunity to share in, 16

Chrysostom: *historesai* means "to pay respects," 32; made distinction between *eidein* (to see) and *historesai,* 31

church: Catholic, 4; communion with, 144; divine economy of the one holy catholic, 11; history of, 4; holy catholic, 14; judgment of second century, 3; Methodist, 2; nascent, 3; Peter as center of unity, 85; received power of keys, 76; Roman Catholic, 2, 99; second century, 4–5; the great, 3; the Spirit, 78; universal, 6; universal mission of, 9

church at Smyrna, 17

church historians, in faculty seminar, 132

church history, critical and ecumenical, 136

church in Asia, represented by Polycarp in Rome, 17

church in Corinth: addressed by Clement from 1 Corinthians 1:10–13, 24; advised by church in Rome, 21; also founded by Peter and Paul, 21; besought by Roman bishop from Paul's first letter to Corinth, 23

church in Rome: 13; besought to pray for church in Syria, 18; concordant apostolic witness of Peter and Paul to, 18; exercising authority from its apostolic vocation, 21; responsibility for church in Corinth, 21; 1 Peter from, 17; Ignatius' letter to, 17; martyrological doctrinal importance, 15; Peter and Paul's leadership roles and martyrdoms in, 135; post-Neronian, 13

church in Syria, prayer for, 18

church of Africa, 74–75, 80

church of Antioch, Peter first bishop, 112

church of Carthage, martyrs in, 77

church of Christ, realization of, 127

church of Corinth, foundation for, 75

church of first Christian millenium, 135

church of Jerusalem, Peter chief of twelve, 112

church of martyrs, 13

church of Rhone Valley in Gaul, bishop of, 114–15

church of Rome: 1–2, 4, 13, 99; active role for other churches, 60; and earlier Christian community in Rome, 105; apostles "poured their whole teaching along with their blood" (Tertullian, *Pre* 36.3), 103–4; apostolic origin, 60; authority as church of Peter, 81; communion with by Protestants, 129; custodian of burial sites, 105; evangelical model for all churches, 104; faith and martyrdom, 118–19; founded by Peter and Paul, 112; "founded" by Peter and Paul's apostolic teaching and martyrdom, 99; importance of, 107, 116; jointly founded by Peter and Paul, 99; living tradition in, 114; normativity of, 81, 117; of martyrs Peter and Paul, 104; penetration by consummated kingdom, 96; Peter associated with, 110; Petrine heritage, 117; presence of Peter and Paul, 119–20; representation of universal church, 60; special place in holy catholic church, 105–6; theological importance of, 107; tradition of, 115; two apostolic burial places give it universal Christian appeal as memorial, 104; vulnerable, 119; faith and hope of, 14; and eastern traditions, 127; apostolic heritage of, 127; authority in church of Corinth because of concordant deaths of Peter and Paul in Rome, 25; "Catholic substance," 127; church of Peter and Paul, 138; church "which dwells in Babylon," 17; consciousness of synoptic gospels, 57; foundation of, 53; founded and built up by Peter and Paul (Irenaeus, *Ag. Her.* 3.3.3), 51; founded by Peter and Paul, 82; fullness of

apostolicity, 64; importance in foundation by martyrs, 84; importance to Tertullian, 72; intention of, 129; martyrdom and leadership of Peter and Paul, 89; martyrdom in Rome and leadership of, 82; mission consists in bearing witness to and living out of united witness of apostles Peter and Paul, 11; normative role for universal church, 65; normativity of, 68; Peter and Paul founders, 85; Petrine-Pauline roots of, 138; presence and influence of Peter and Paul in, 73; prominence of, 9; protected, strengthened, and ruled by Peter and Paul, 5; role of Paul for, 141; the interpreting activity of, 129; theological importance for Irenaeus, 57; three apostles martyred, 72; under constraint to remember founding by Peter and Paul, 11; unique authority of, 72

church of second century, 3
church of today, continuity/identity with church of apostles, 96–97
church order, Peter as foundation, 76
church universal, 1
churches, apostolic origin of, 59
churches, Pauline, addressed by 1 Peter, 7
churches from Asia Minor, exclusion by bishop of Rome, 114
churches in Asia Minor, exclusion of, 115
churches of Asia and Phrygia, peace on, 143
churches of Asia Minor, threat of excommunication, 65

churches of Christ in Judea, Paul
    unknown by face to, 28
churches of Galatia, letter by Paul
    of his trip to Jerusalem three
    years after his conversion to
    visit Peter, 28
church's tradition, development
    of, 81
church's tradition, important key
    in understanding scriptures, 3
Cilicia. *See* Syria and Cilicia
Cilician gates, Paul moves north
    from Syria toward Galatia, 29
Clement of Rome: 4, 21, 139;
    employs 1 Corinthians 1:10–13
    for problem in Corinth, 24;
    writing from the church of
    Paul's martyrdom, 24
Clement's intervention, more
    understandable in light of
    Paul's emissary (Timothy), 25
college of bishops and apostles, 91
collegial consensus, 125
collegial consensus and personal
    initiative, pope's role, 88
collegial relationship, martyr
    apostles Peter and Paul, 129
collegiality: inclusion of
    Orthodox, 129; nature of
    episcopal, 136; Peter and Paul,
    124
colleagueship between Protestants
    and Roman Catholics,
    academic, 99
common ground, 2
common witness, 13
communicatores, 143–44
concordant, spirit, 133
concordant deaths of Paul and
    Peter in Rome, authority with
    which church in Rome
    addresses church in Corinth, 25
confessor, martyr designate, 144
Congar, Y. M. J., 1, 131, 138,
    146–147, 149, 150

consensus: limited and
    provisional, 2; not yet, 126
constitutive, Paul's martyrdom
    as, 24
constitutive event, 14
"continuity," crucial in
    ecumenical church history, 131
convergence of views, Roman
    Catholics and Protestants, 121
conversatio, conduct, 69
conversion, of Paul, 6, 34
Corinth: 25; colony of Rome, 21;
    Dionysius of, 4
Corinthian Christians, addressed
    from Roman martyrological
    tradition, 25
Corinthian church, *See* church in
    Corinth
Corinthian church: 50; Paul's
    tradition of Lord's supper, 26;
    problems facing, 26
Corinthians, "bought at a price,"
    18
corpus, Pauline, dominating
    second half of canon, 7
Council of Ephesus, presence of
    Peter and Paul, 94
Council of Jerusalem,
    concordance of Peter and Paul,
    136
Council of Nicea, 142
counter-reformation, 111
creator God, Jesus as Christ of,
    72
cross, Peter's refusal of, 8
cult of the apostles, absent in
    Protestantism, 120
cult of Peter and Paul, at San
    Sebastiano in third century, 92–
    93
cultural diversity, wide limits of,
    136
Currie, Stewart Dickson, 139–40
Cyprian: 76, 141; and apostates,
    145; concerning Peter, 81

Cyril of Alexandria, agreement with John of Antioch, 93

Damascus: 40; before and after Paul's time in Arabia, 29
Damian, Peter, 147
date of Easter, issue between churches of Asia Minor and Rome, 114
day of martyrdom. *See* martyrdom, day of
Dead Sea, 41
death, faithful obedience unto, 25
Decian persecution, 145
decrees of Roman magisterium, with typical Pauline phrase (Gal 1:8–9), 4
Decretum Gelasianum, Roman primacy, 83
defined dogma, 3
Demoustier, A., 143
Denzinger, H., 147
Deusdedit (cardinal), presence of Peter and Paul, 93
"development," crucial in ecumenical church history, 131
"Development of catholic Christianity in the Second Century," field of inquiry, 132
development of New Testament canon, 4
devil, the Christian's enemy, 17
dia ten hikanoteran archen, original of *propter potentiorem principalitatem,* "because of its most (or more) excellent origin," 59
dialogue, vii
Dilthey, origins of ecumenical church history, 131
Dionysius, bishop of Alexandria, letter to Fabius, bishop of Rome, 53, 77, 144–45
Dionysius of Corinth, 4

disciple of the Twelve, Paul not, 36
disciples, seventy, 54
diversity, breadth and limits of, 134
divine constraint, 11
divine economy of the one holy catholic church, 11
doctor, Paul's primacy, 134
doctrinal agreement of Peter and Paul, 4
doctrinal purity, theoretical questions about, 135
doctrine, authority and agreement of Peter and Paul, 80
doctrine of martyrdom, based on bodily suffering of Christ, 16
doctrine of participation, used by Tertullian, 81
dogma: Catholic, 9; defined, 3; official, 3; reintegrating of, 3; Roman Catholic, 2
dogmatic statement, 3
Domitian and Severans, epoch between, 132
Donfried, K. P., 138
Donovan, M. A., 140
Doutreleau, L., 58, 140
Dov-Neeman, 139

Early Catholic Christianity, Seminar on Development of, vii
early patristic view, 107
Easter controversy, test case of authority of church of Rome, 65
eastern churches, concerning Peter, 81
ecclesia Petri propinqua, 145
ecclesia rather than *thiasos,* 132
ecclesiastical authority, integrity of, 125
ecclesiastical calendar, 114

ecclesiology of holy catholic
    church, 115
ecclesiology of Paul, 75
ecumenical church history: 130;
    aim at respect and dialogue,
    131; credible narratives rather
    than triumphalism, 131
ecumenical convergences,
    prospects for, 135
ecumenical council of church,
    first (Gal 2:1-10), 110
ecumenical dialogue: vii, 1, 10;
    resource of great import in, 136
ecumenical discussion, 9
ecumenical *experience,* in faculty
    seminar, 132
ecumenical future, use in, 137
ecumenical protocol, 117-18
ecumenical research, vii
ecumenical scene in America, 1
ecumenical task, 3
Edinburgh (1910), 135
Eleutherus, bishop, 58
Empie, P. C., 138
England, missionary thrust to, 10,
    88
Ephesus, "luminaries" in, 66
episcopacy, fullness of, 76
episcopate, Peter and Paul hand
    over the ministry of the, 4
episcopus episcoporum, term of
    mockery, 78
eschata, presence of, 150
eschatological discourse of Jesus,
    exhortation to martyrdom
    (Matt 24:9-14) in, 104
eucharist: celebration of, 68;
    discussed by Paul (1 Cor 10:16-
    17), 26
eucharistic meal, pilgrims and
    bishop of Rome, 114
European scholarship, 1
Eusebius: 144; Easter controversy,
    66; paschal controversy, 142
evangellion, does not mean
    "information about Jesus," 32

evidence, early patristic, 9
eyewitness, night in which Jesus
    was delivered up, 27
ex cathedra, 3
excommunication, from tombs
    and presence of Peter and Paul,
    67
expediting the gospel, motivated
    Paul in concern for truth about
    resurrection of Jesus, 27

Fabius, bishop of Rome, letter
    from Dionysius, 144
faith: apostolic, 119; apostolic
    witness of the holy catholic, 17;
    tested through suffering, 71;
    truth of the apostolic, 11;
    understanding in the, vii; unity
    of the, vii
faith of apostles as celebrated in
    Asia, brought by Polycarp to
    Rome, 17
faith of Christians, being tested
    through trial and persecution, 8
faith of Peter, in later fathers, 146
faithful from everywhere
    (Irenaeus, *Ag. Her.* 3.3.2), 5, 11,
    113
"free men," 5
faithful obedience unto death,
    subsequent connotation of "Be
    ye imitators of me" (1 Cor
    4:16), 25
Farkasfalvy, Denis M., O. Cist.,
    140, 150
Farmer, William R., vii, 134-36,
    139-40, 150; bishop of Rome's
    freedom of action, 125;
    development of Roman canon,
    57; insights and expositions of,
    137; Peter as mediator, 122-23;
    relationship between Peter and
    Paul, 122
fasting, differences in, 68
Father, source of knowledge,
    55

Father and Son, dialectical relationship in revealing activity, 55
feast of Peter and Paul, homily of Paul VI on, 89
fellowship, handshake of, 6, 9
Ferguson, E., 146
fifteen days, Paul's visit with Peter in Jerusalem, 28
First and second Peter, suggesting Petrine control over Pauline churches and writings, 7
First Clement: 53; cited Peter and Paul as examples of apostles who "contended even unto death," 20
First Corinthians: 24–27; central message as gospel of crucified and risen Christ, 24; Paul received tradition "that Christ died for our sins, in accordance with the scriptures," 34
First Corinthians 11:23–26, origin and significance in relationship of Peter and Paul, 26
First Peter: 7, 15, 112: apostolic letter from Rome, 17
five hundred brethren, 27
"flesh and blood," Paul did not immediately confer with, 28–29
Florovsky, Georges, church historian, 131
"for fifteen days," 28
formation of New Testament canon, presupposes Peter and Paul's dual leadership of post-conciliar church (Gal. 2:7–9) and their subsequent concordant martyrdom, 48
foundation of church, Peter through confession of faith, 86
"founding" by Peter and Paul, 146
founding of church of Rome, Peter along with Paul, 112; Peter and Paul, 59

fourteen years, 6, 29
fourth century, 4
fourth gospel, in canon only with appendix affirming Peter as chief shepherd, 7
Franciscans, 10
freedom in Christ: attained through suffering, 18; cover for hubris, 128
freedman of Jesus Christ, 17–18
fundamentalist position, 97

Galatia. See churches of Galatia
Galatians: (letter) 6, 28–39; 140; (addressees) uninformed of Paul's earliest contacts with Jerusalem-based apostles, 29
Galatia, Paul in new phase of missionary work, 29
Garrett, James Leo, Jr., 139
Gaul: Irenaeus bishop in, 13; Irenaeus from, 14
Gelasian Decree, 147
Gentiles: admitted into Church without being subjected to law of Moses, 6; apostle to, 50, 86; apostle to: see apostle to Gentiles; missionary for, 9; Paul's apostolic mission to, 6–7; Paul's westward mission to, 30
Gentiles in Rome, martyrdom of Peter and Paul not solely for, 104
Gerhardsson, Birger, 139
gloriosissimis, 62
gnosis, full knowledge, 54
gnostics: disagreement among, 64–65; disagreement in opposition to unanimity of faith of Church, 65; teachings of, 64
God: communion with, 145; purpose of, 119
God the Father, eternal shepherd, 91

God's plan: 8; Peter's role as "rock" in, 75
God's revelation, 3
good shepherd, lays down his life for his sheep, 8
gospel: 9; atoning power of, 13; died for, 13; Paul's as implicit canon of New Testament, 10; with martyrdoms, 105; *see* normative events of gospel.
gospel of Matthew: 46, 111; guarantee by Peter and Paul, 57; pro-Petrine tradition (Matt 16:17–19), 109–10
gospel of crucified and risen Christ, undergirded by normative authority of Isaiah 53, 24
gospels of Mark and Luke, legitimized, 56
gospel teaching, "where two or three are gathered," 120
governing by apostles, prayer not juridical, 91
grace, God's, 119
Granfield, P., 151
great church in second century, 3
"great luminaries," 66
Greek Fathers, 141
Greek geographers, beginnings of "history," 30
Greek historians, at first geographers of rivers and seas, 30; questioned priests of remote cultures about records in temples, 30
Gregory I, 124
Gregory VII, 149

harmony, 5
he archaia paradosis, the original tradition, 60
hegemonikon, principal, ruling, leading, 59
Hellenistic culture, Christianity's stabilizations within, 132

Henry IV, 149
heresies, errors of, 54
heresy: 13; father of, 59
heretic, 4, 12
heritage: (Peter's) confession of faith and witness, 86; joint Petrine-Pauline, 2; Pauline, 10; Petrine and Pauline, 129
heritage of Peter and Paul, bishop of Rome's vocation, 87
hermeneutical chasms, bridge over, 132
hidryo, to found, 61
hierarchical order, juridical questions about, 135
hierarchy, activity of, 96
Higgins, A. J. B., 139
hikanoteran, 141
Hilary of Poitiers, 146
histor, judge, examiner and arbiter in legal matters in ancient Greece, 30
historesai (Gal 1:18): helps to establish Paul's apostolic independence and his apostolic authority, 36; to inquire into or about a thing, or to inquire about a person, or to examine or observe, 30
historia, "inquiry," etc., 139
historical critical method, 97
historical inquiry, of great import, 136
"history," begun by Greek geographers, 30
history of the church, 4
holy catholic church: 98–99; apostolic faith of, 119; ecclesiology of, 115; exclusion from, 114; life of, 114; local churches of, 124; Petrine heritage, 117; Protestants and church of Rome, 129; special place of church of Rome in, 105–6
Holy See, decrees of, 148

Holy Spirit: assistance of, 119; gifts of, 136; in martyr, 144; inspiration of, 144; ministry of apostles through bishops, 92; prayer of, 144; teaching inspired by, 62; transcendent principle of unity and interiority, 97

homologous structures, practical questions about, 135

Hungarian, 130

Hungary, missionary thrust to, 10, 88

"identity," crucial in ecumenical church history, 131

Ignatius: 4–5, 139, 148; beseeches prayer by the church in Rome for church in Syria, 18; climax of letter to Rome, 18; exercise authority by love, 21; imitating Paul's words, 18–19; knows of concordant apostolic witness of Peter and Paul to church in Rome, 18; letter to Romans, 17, 53; martyr as "the word of God," 63

Illyricum, before Paul's letter to Rome he never preached west of, 101

incarnate Son, Irenaeus' emphasis, 55

infallibility, pope's, 110

infallibility of universal church, 2

influence, Pauline (or rather deutero-Pauline), 7

Innocent III, 10

inquiry, distinctive spirit of, 130

Irenaeus: 2, 4, 12, 115–16, 134, 136, 140, 148; agreement of Peter and Paul, 53–54; apostles and heretics, 142; bridge between churches of Asia Minor and west, 58; Christ of Paul not gnostic, 56;

development of theme of shared leadership by, 133; equality of Peter and Paul, 80; experienced faith and hope of church in Rome, 14; "faithful from everywhere," 105; perception of church of Rome consonant with New Testament regarding Peter and Paul, 52; Peter and Paul and importance of church of Rome, 57; Peter and Paul and synoptic gospels, 57; Peter and Paul founding church of Rome not from pagan myths and legends, 103; Peter and Paul martyr founders, 72; Peter and Paul's involvement with church in Rome provided holy catholic church with touchstone in history for combating heretics, 48; "primitive" traditions, 98; Rome's position in Easter controversy, 68; same dignity for Peter and Paul, 68; theological synthesis, 54; tradition coming from apostles was always preserved in Rome, 14

Irenaeus and Tertullian, theology of, 80

irenic discourse, shared universe of, 136

Isaiah 9:1–2, key text for understanding composition of Matthew, 41

Isaiah 53: atoning death and resurrection of Christ, 6; background of 1 Corinthians 15:3, 50

Italy, 13

James: church authority in Jerusalem at Paul's visit, 28; Jerusalem apostle, 122; not comparable to Peter as

informant concerning Jesus' teaching and ministry, 32
James, Peter and John, 6
Jansenist opinion, condemned in 1647, 148
Jerome: 146; reference to Tertullian, 143
Jerusalem: 6–7, 13; church authorities in, 28; conference in, 7; location of Lord's supper, 50; meeting in, 7; Paul in danger in, 14; Paul leaves for Syria and Cilicia, 29; Paul's martyrdom in Rome emanating from, 14; Paul's mission begins in, 7–8; Paul's service for (Rom 15.31), 100; scriptural precedence of Rome, 14; visit proceeded from three years of preaching and decision on Gentile mission, 30
Jerusalem agreement, 7
Jerusalem and Rome, Paul witnessed to Jesus in, 7
Jerusalem conference, possible because Peter arranged it at Paul's request?, 47
Jerusalem handshake: collegial unity, 124; of fellowship between Peter and Paul, 9
Jesus: 8, 140; advises followers against "lording it over" one's subjects, 21; apostles and disciples of, 53; assurance that he originated the tradition concerning Lord's Supper as handed down by Paul, 26; earthly ministry and Peter, 125; first appearance to Peter, 110–11; followed by Peter into martyrdom, 8; instituted martyrological church living out of his atoning sacrifice, 51; martyrological tradition of, 102; "master of martyrdom," 62;

origin of tradition concerning Lord's Supper, 50; Peter's beliefs about the meaning of Jesus' death and resurrection, 33; Peter's confession of faith in, 86; Peter's continuing mission of, 8; Peter's memory of and belief about, 33; rebuke of Peter, 109; reign through death and crucifixion, 95; risen, 33; teaching and ministry, 33; virginal conception, 55–56
Jesus and Peter, participation between, 75
Jesus and the Christ, not separate, 55
Jesus Christ: atoning sacrifice of, 119; center of unity, 110; foundation, 75; instituted rite celebrating fulfillment of law and prophets and appropriating redemption, 51; life etc., 119; Peter and Paul's common witness to, 9; revelation of, 34; "attained to" by Ignatius through suffering, 18
Jesus of Nazareth and risen Lord, bishop witnesses to, 87
Jewish matrix, Christianity's emergence from, 132
Johannine writings, presence in church of Rome, 73
John: 66; apostle, 68; confession of faith of, 73; confessor, 72; disciple of Lord, 56, 67; martyr in Rome, 72; quasi-martyrdom in Rome, 81; sojourn and boiling in oil, 73
John XXIII: 125; convocation of Vatican II, 125; liberated forces of renewal by convoking Vatican II, 10; renewal in Vatican II, 88
John and James: complementary to Peter and Paul, 53–54;

mentioned with Peter and Paul, 80

John Chrysostom, 146

John of Antioch, agreement with Cyril of Alexandria, 93

joint founding, church of Rome by Peter and Paul, 99

joint martyrdom. *See* martyrdom, joint

joint martyrdom of Peter and Paul in Rome, 4

joint Petrine-Pauline heritage, 2

joint role of Peter and Paul, theological significance of, 53

Jones, Henry Stuart, 139

Jordan River, 40

Judea: churches of Christ in, 28; unbelievers in (Rom 15:31), 100

judging: bishop's eschatological act of, 95; explanation in liturgy, 90

judgment, apostles Peter and Paul sit in Rome, 4

judgment of second-century church, 3

judgment over church, by martyrs presently, 90

jurisdiction: of bishop of Rome, 113; of pope, 110

kathedra, location of teaching, 94–95

Kereszty, Roch, O. Cist.: vii, 98–99, 105, 108, 133–36; bishop of Rome, 118; bishop of Rome and episcopal college, 125; Chapter 3, 113, 116; Chapter 4, 107, 116; conclusion of Irenaeus discussion, 116–17; implications of papal supremacy and infallibility, 107; importance of Peter, 118; insights and exposition of, 137; intercession for church of

Rome, 120; martyrdom, 119–20; papal supremacy and infallibility, 107; Peter as center, 111; Peter and papacy, 109; Peter's call, 123; pope and unity of church, 115; power to exclude, 115; synoptic gospels and John's appendix, 123

key in understanding scriptures, church's tradition, 3

"key of doctrine," 76

keys to kingdom, Peter as recipient, 76

Kilpatrick, G. D.: 31, 33; Paul did not "inquire into, investigate" *(historesai)* Cephas, 32–33; concludes that *historesai* at Galatians 1:18 means "to get information from Cephas," 31–32; theory about Paul's visit of Peter, 32

kingdom: consummation through Jesus and apostles, 95–96; final coming in future, 90; God's, 119; imminent arrival of, 95

kingdom of heaven, keys to, 76

koinonia: handshake of, 6; of "separated brothers and sisters," 134; visible, 135

koryphaios, 141

kyrios, Christ as only, 90

Lake of Galilee, 40

Lanne, E., 58, 62, 64, 67, 138, 140, 142

Latin America, missionary thrust to, 10, 88

Latin commentators, agree with Chrysostom on *historesai,* 31

law, area of expertise of Greek *histor,* 30

law of Moses, Gentiles not subjected to, 6

Leo X, 149

lexicographers, *historesai* (Gal

1:18) as "*visit* a person *(Cephas)* for the purpose of inquiry," 31

Liddell, Henry George, 139

Liddell and Scott: 33; article on *historesai,* 31; *historesai* means "to visit a person for purpose of inquiry," 32

life, new in Christ, 5

Lightfoot, J. B., 139

Linus: bishop, 58; Peter and Paul hand over ministry of episcopate to, 4

literature, "apostolic," 3

liturgical prayers, 4

liturgy: preserving awareness of both Peter and Paul as patrons of church of Rome and authorities for pope, 4; testimony of intercession of saints, 92; witness of, 9

local church, relation to Peter's church, 78

local church of city of Rome, 114

local churches, equal, 124

"logos theou," martyr in suffering, 90

Loi, V., 142

Lord's supper: 6; taken up by Paul in 1 Corinthians, 26; tradition concerning, 50

Ludwig: 74, 141, 143, 145; traditional Catholic exegesis (Irenaeus, *Ag. Her.* 3.3.2), 61

Luke, follower of Paul, 56

Luther: 149; activity of apostles continuing, 120

magisterium: reaffirmation of ancient tradition by, 84; Roman, 4

Manson, Thomas Walter, 139

March, W. Eugene, 140

Marcion: 142; refutation by Tertullian, 69

Marcionites: 54; wrong, 72

Mark, disciple and interpreter of Peter, 56

martyr, Christian, 16

martyr: keys, 77; testimony of Christ through, 89

martyr apostles: reign with Jesus through death, 95; Peter and Paul, 11

martyrdom: 6; and apostolic mission, 82; of Peter and Paul, 5, 8; Christian perfection in Irenaeus, 62; constitutive of foundation of Rome by Peter and Paul, 81; constitutive of leadership, 107; day of, 5; doctrine based on Christ's bodily suffering, 16; dominical exhortation to (Matt 10:16–22; 24:9–14), 104; experience of, 114; guarantee of gospel witness, 72; in city of Rome, 82; jointly of Peter and Paul, 4–5; Paul's in Rome, 7, 14; Paul's in Rome in martyrological tradition from Jerusalem, 14; Peter's, 112; Peter's as actual consummation of his "office" as representing chief shepherd Jesus, 8; spiritual power through, 105; systematic theology, 119–20; theological connection with apostleship, 9

martyrdom of Peter, patristic texts on, 53

martyrdom of Peter and Paul: 13, 105; constitutive of apostolic mission, 89; import not restricted to Rome or Gentiles in Rome, 104; in continuity with atoning sacrifice of Jesus, 51; in 1 Clement 5, 20–23

martyrdom of Peter and Paul in Rome: 100, 103; constitutive of church, 14 martyrdom of the apostle Paul, memory of, 13

martyrdom of the apostle Peter, memory of, 13

martyrdom of the apostles Peter and Paul, 13

martyrdom of two chief apostles of church, examples of obedience unto death in accordance with Jesus' apostolic commission (Matt 10:16–23), 102–3

martyrdoms of Peter and Paul, 105

martyrdoms: apostolic, 104–5; Peter and Paul, 113

martyresai: 14; Paul's in Rome, 7

martyrological tradition: in 1 Peter, 15; of Jesus, 102

martyrs: against pagan philosophers, 71; canon of, 13; church of, 13; connection with Jesus in death, 90; participation of, 144; restoration of sinners, 77; role similar to bishop and church, 144

martyrs of Vienne and Lyons, letter of, 77

Mary Magdalene and other Mary, 46

master martyr, 13

"master of martyrdom," Jesus, 62

Matthean-Petrine and Pauline terminology, in Irenaeus, 61

Matthew (evangelist), 56, 139

Matthew (gospel), 139

McCord, P. J., 138

Melito of Sardis, 66

Menander, 142

Methodist church, 2

Miletus, Paul's sermon (Acts 20:18–38) in, 7

Miller, J. M., 138

ministry, Petrine, 1

Missale Romanum, common feast of Peter and Paul, 84

mission: apostolic, 5, 8; universal, 9

mission of church of Rome, consists in bearing witness to and living out of united witness of Peter and Paul, 11

missionary and inspired theologian, superiority of Paul as, 133

modern historical consciousness, rise of, 131

Mohlberg, K., 148

Mohrmann, C., 142

monogamous, married only once, 143

montanism, 143

Montanist Tertullian, polemics of, 77

Moses' seat, Paul sat in as Pharisee, 35

Mother Teresa, 88

movements, charismatic, 10

Murphy, T. A., 138

mutuality, vii

mystery: Christian, *See* Christian mystery; full knowledge of, 54

Naphtali, land of, 42

nascent church, 3

New English Bible, 33

"new prophecy," 143

New Testament: 1, 5–6, 8–9, 14, 107, 110–11; apostolic faith in, 128; apostolic witness of Peter and Paul embodied in, 10; composition of some of books of, 14; development of canon, 4; foundations for understanding ecumenical importance of church of Rome, 12; given by pre-Constantinian church, 120; implicit canon of, 10; martyrdom of Peter and

Paul and, 82; no "Petrine primacy" over Paul, 122; Paul's authority in, 128; Petrine text in, 117

New Testament books, composition of, 6

New Testament canon: 3, 11, 140; formation of, 14

New Testament experts, in faculty seminar, 132

New Testament scholar, 130

Nicholas I: 147, 149; authority of Peter and Paul, 83, 133; letter to Emperor Michael III of Byzantium, 84

night in which Jesus was delivered up, Paul not eyewitness, 27

Nisan, fourteenth day of, 65

normative events of gospel, Paul's care in certifying, 27

normativity of church of Rome, 81

obedience unto death, 105

obedient unto death, 13

observers, Protestant and Orthodox at Vatican II, 126

oikoumene: 102; root-meaning of, 136

opponents of Paul (2 Cor), 49

organic unity: definitions of, 136; primal image of, 136

Origen: 4, 80, 146; development by, 133

Orthodox: 3; authority of Rome, 125

orthodox churches, patriarchs of, 117

Orthodox dialogue partners, inclusion of, 129

Orthodox theologians: participation of, 121; unity (ecumenical), 120

"our common history as Christians," Third World Conference of Faith and Order, 131

Outler, Albert C., vii

Pagels, E. H., 140

papacy, and preservation of apostolic faith, 127

papal power, unchecked freedom of, 125

pardon for sins, 144

parousia, expectation faded, 90

Pascha, fourteenth of, 66

paschal controversy, 142

patristic age, 4

patristic and liturgical tradition, 3

patristic literature, 1

patristic theology, 9

patristic view: 5; martyrdom of Peter and Paul, 82

patrologist and theologian, 130

Paul: vii, 7, 140; action with authority, 128; and handling of churches, 128; "apostle to Gentiles," 86; apostolic claims of, 133; apostolic independence, 33; apostolic mission to Gentiles acknowledged by James, Peter and John, 6; apostolic power of, 24; apostolic preaching consummated, increased to universal dimensions, and perpetuated through his final act of witnessing, 9; apostolic presence in Corinth, 25; appeals to his own example, 26; arguing for his independence of authority of Jerusalem apostles, 33; as a Pharisee sat in Moses' seat, 35; at Christ's "right hand," 134; at right of Jesus, 147; authority from risen Christ, 86; authority in charismatic foresight and theological depth, 51; authority of, 24; belief that resurrection appearances to Peter and other apostles were of same order as Paul's, 27; call to Gentiles, 122; came to Rome, 99; charisms subordinate to apostolic authority of, 148; Christian leader, 35; Christ's appearance, 34; communion with pillars of church, 86; concern for truth of traditions received from church of Peter, 6; concern to "get it right" is foundational to Christian life and faith, 36; contact with church authorities in Jerusalem, 28; contemplative life, 133; conversion, 29, 34; Corinthians "bought at a price," 18; death, 8; and practical problems in Corinthian church, 25; discussion of resurrection appearances with Peter, 27; *doctor* (teacher), 86; *doctrina* (theological teaching), 86; dominating second half of Acts, 7; enforcer of Torah, 35; example in encouraging, testing, and coordinating charisms in church, 10; fifteen days with Peter, 6; first trial, 8; founder, 141; Galatians uninformed of Paul's earliest contacts with Jerusalem-based apostles, 29; groundwork for westward mission to Gentiles laid during three year interval, 30; heritage of, 10; his first letter to Corinthians employed in 1 Clement 47, 23; his gospel as implicit canon of New Testament, 10; his martyrdom as constitutive of church, 24; his persecution of Christians

could have been along road running by Capernaum on way from Judea and Galilee to Damascus, 44; his statement that he remained with Peter fifteen days is important, since his purpose would have been better served could he have said he remained only one day, 37–39; in danger in Jerusalem, 14; in Irenaeus, 141; influence to "all the nations," 9; letters, 140; Marcion interpretation of, 70; Roman martyrdom and birth, 92; martyrdom in Rome, 14; memory of martyrdom of apostle, 13; mission beginning in Jerusalem and concluding with preaching ministry in Rome, 7–8; mission of, 9; made innocuous social visit with Peter?, 31; most of over five hundred with resurrection appearances still alive (1 Cor 15:6), 27; no need of Peter's knowledge, 32; not critical of Peter concerning Corinthian divisiveness (1 Cor 1:12), 49; did not immediately confer with flesh and blood or contact prior apostles in Jerusalem, 28–29; not subservient in going to Jerusalem to question Peter, 36; opponents in 2 Corinthians, 49; had opportunity to discuss Lord's supper tradition with eyewitness apostles, 50; overall argument in Galatians, 36; partnership with Peter when he began preaching faith he once ravished (Gal 1:23)?, 45; passed on pro-Petrine tradition which developed in a church with an incipient Petrine primacy, 46–47; passed on tradition received from eyewitnesses?, 50; passed on tradition received from mission Peter led?, 45; passed on traditions received from church he had persecuted, 27; permanent connection with Rome, 73; persecuted church, 27; persecuting activity in Damascus or southern Syria, 29; persecutor of church and acquainted with gospel preached in church, 34; Peter's word on resurrection appearances and the appearance to Paul, 27; Pharisee of Pharisees, 34; preached gospel in area of former persecuting activity outside Judea during three year period, 29; preached gospel prior to fifteen day visit with Peter, 45; pre-Christian, 34; pre-Christian questioning focused on interpretation of law and prophets, 35; preparation for mission, 35; purpose in history making trip to Jerusalem, 28; questions eyewitnesses who first formed tradition he is passing on, 36; rebuke of Peter, 128; received "the gospel" by revelation (Gal 1:11–12), 32; role for church of Rome, 141; role ignored, 61; seeing risen Jesus gives equal footing with other apostles, 33; seeks information of eyewitness and disciple Peter and not James, 32; sees Jesus as Son of God, 34; special position of, 86; subordinate to Peter in Tertullian's *Against Marcion,* 70, 80; superior to Peter, 147; technical terminology for traditions, 27; terminology in

Irenaeus, 61; "thirteenth apostle," 86; three-year period between return to Damascus and visit with Peter, 28; to Jerusalem, 143; to Jerusalem to visit Peter (Gal 1:18), 31; "to visit" or "to get to know," 28; traditions whose truth he considered central to preaching, 6; his understanding of gospel was normative, 10; witness of him in Ignatius, 17; witness to power of risen Lord, 87; witnessed to Jesus in Jerusalem and Rome, 7; words imitated by Ignatius, 18–19; writings and theology in New Testament, 86–87; zealous for law, 35

Paul VI: foundation of Rome by Peter and Paul, 84; Homily on feast of Saints Peter and Paul, 150; interventions of, 125; pope, 125, 148; prayers of Peter and Paul, 95; reflection of Peter and Paul, 89; Second Vatican Council, 133

Paul and Barnabas, pillars united with, 110

Pauline, 4

Pauline ecclesiology, Jesus as rock and foundation, 81

Pauline heritage: bishop of Rome and, 87; universal mission and concern for truth, 117

Pauline letters, gnostic exegesis of, 140

Paul's emissary, helps in understanding Clement's intervention, 25

Paul's inquiry, focus on Jesus and Peter's credibility, 33

Paul's vocation: personal charism, 87; showing freedom of God's grace, 87 *peccata capitalia,* forgiveable by prophet or apostle, 145

Pelikan, Jaroslav, church historian, 131

penance, ecclesiastical character of, 78

penitents, reconciliation of, 144

period of Irenaeus and Tertullian, 99

persecution: consolation and inspiration in, 112; imperial 13; Neronian, 13–14, 133; opportunity for Christian martyr to share in Christ's suffering, 16; Paul in Damascus or southern Syria, 29; resistance to imperial, 15

perspective: Protestant, 98; Roman Catholic, 98

Peter: vii, 1; apostle cited with Paul in 1 Clement 5, 20; apostolic commission, 141; apostolic mission to circumcised, 6; appears as first bishop of Rome only in third century, 4; as rock, 8; associated with church of Rome, 112; authoritative action, 128; authority over koinonia of faith of apostles and as chief shepherd, 51; bishop of Rome as successor of, 2, 83; called Satan, 125; came to Rome, 99; center of unity, 85; chief guarantor of tradition of Jesus and leader of twelve in synoptic gospels, 7; chief shepherd in fourth gospel, 7; church of (Jerusalem), 6; church of Rome and, 110; committing a fault, 143; continuing mission of Jesus, 8; cooperation with Paul, 122; divinely appointed CEO, 133; dominating first half of Acts, 7;

evangelization of Gentiles, 122; eyewitness and disciple of Jesus, 32; eyewitness of earthly life of Jesus and risen Christ, 6; first apostle or bishop, 81; first bishop, 76; first bishop of Antioch, 106; first Gentile mission, 148; first witness of risen Christ and chief shepherd, 147–48; foundation and agent, 76; foundation for universal church, 74; foundation of church of Rome, 53; good shepherd, 123; heritage of, 10; his memory of and his belief about Jesus, 33; holding key to right interpretation of Pauline corpus according to 2 Peter, 7; importance of credibility as witness, 33; interpretation of Paul, 123; keys to kingdom, 76; leadership position of, 141; leading role of, 70; martyrdom of, 53; mediator between Paul and earlier apostles, 122–23; memory of martyrdom of apostle, 13; ministry of, 9; ministry through bishop of Rome, 94; not first bishop of Rome, 4; office from faith, 148; Paul had no need of Peter's knowledge, 32; Paul superior to, 147; Pauline literary genre of apostolic letter attributed to, 7; Paul's call, 122–23; pope's relation to, 110; presence with bishop of Rome, 93; price of freedom is blood of Christ, 18; *principatus* (primacy), 86; received innocuous social visit from Paul?, 31; risk in agreeing to meeting with Paul, 36; risk in receiving Paul great but justified by Christian faith, 36; rock, 80; rock as foundation for

Church, 76; role as leading
apostle conditioned on
acceptance of cross, 8; Rome as
first see of, 83; title for, 141; to
Rome, 8; view of Paul's coming
to Jerusalem unknown, 36;
visited by Paul in Jerusalem
(Gal. 1:18), 30; witness, 33:
witness of him in Ignatius, 18;
witness to earthly life and
passion of Jesus, 87; writing
from "Babylon," 8
Peter and John, eyewitness
apostles at Lord's supper, 50
Peter and papacy, connection
between, 85
Peter and Paul: vii, 1–2, 4;
agreement in Tertullian, 69;
agreement of, 6; agreement
with prophets, 54; ambivalent
relationships between, 133; and
founders Romulus and Remus,
83; and normativity of church
of Rome, 81; apostolic
martyrdom of, 5; apostolic
source of Catholic faith, 84;
apostolic witness embodied in
New Testament, 10;
appearances of risen Lord to, 6;
authority and agreement in
doctrine, 80; authority of, 36,
82; both founding apostles, 5;
burial sites, 105; Christ-like
examples of martyred apostles,
15; collegial authority, 124;
collegial relationship of martyr
apostles, 129; complementary
roles, 133; concordant deaths
of, 25; concordant witness in
apostolic tradition in Asia
before Polycarp's visit to
Rome, 17; concordant witness
normative for Irenaeus was
normed by "truth of gospel,"
48; concordant witness to

church in Rome known by
Ignatius, 18; conflict over
conduct not preaching, 69;
disagreements between, 136;
doctrinal agreement of, 4; dual
mandate from Christ, 110;
equal in Tertullian's
Prescription against Heretics,
70; equality in Irenaeus, 80;
equality of, 82; equivalent
apostolic status, 135; faith and
blood, 118–19; "fathers" of
Rome, 83; foundation and
martyrdom of, 73; foundation
of church of Rome by both, 9;
founded church in Corinth, 21;
founded church of Rome and
sealed their joint witnessing by
their joint martyrdom, 5;
founders for Irenaeus, 72;
founders of church of Rome,
59, 82, 104, 106, 110, 117;
founding church of Rome, 103;
free men in Ignatius, 63;
guarantors of synoptic gospels,
57; hand over ministry of
episcopate to Linus, 4; heritage
of, 126; importance of
relationship between them for
understanding 1 Corinthians
11:23–26, 26; influence in
shepherding and teaching by
bishop of Rome, 96; inspiring
examples of, 13; Jerusalem
agreement of, 87; joint
importance, 107; joint
martyrdom of, 5; joint
martyrdom in Rome, 4; martyr
apostles, 11, 123; martyrdom,
8, 13, 103, 105, 119–20, 133;
martyrdom and leadership of
church of Rome, 89;
martyrdom and mission, 89;
martyrdom in 1 Clement 5, 20–
23; martyrdom in Rome, 14;

martyred, 105; martyred in Antioch, 106; martyrs, 104, 117; memory in liturgy, 84; missions in Rome, 133; organic unity of, 136; partners, 123–24; partnership in apostolic founding and building up of church of Rome (Irenaeus, *Ag. Her.* 3.3.3), 51; partnership in New Testament, 51; patristic texts, 53; patrons of church of Rome and authorities for pope, 4; popes as successors of, 86; post-conciliar tension calls for pre-conciliar solidarity to account for eventual outcome, 49; presence and influence in church of Rome, 73; presence in church of Rome, 94, 119–20; relationship of mutuality, 122; relationship of bishop of Rome to, 11; representative of apostles, 53, 80; role of, 99; roles of, vii; same revelation to, 55, 68; sit in judgment in Rome, 4; suffering martyrdom together in Rome, 9; "supreme power of," 84; teaching of, 140; tension in Corinth between, 49; testimony for synoptic gospels, 56; theological importance of church of Rome connected in Irenaeus, 57; together protect, strengthen, and rule church of Rome, 5; two most glorious apostles, 106; united apostolic authority of, 13; united witness of, 11; unity of Testaments, 54; unity organic, 135; witness of, 129; witness of the two most glorious apostles, 106

Peter and successors, earthly exemplars of heavenly foundation, 134

Peter and twelve, beginning of

series of resurrection appearances, 27

Peter, James and John, dominate Jesus tradition used by evangelist Matthew, 43

Peter, Paul and John, martyr apostles in Rome, 72

"Peter-Paul Syndrome," new ecumenical horizons opened up by, 135

Petrine-Pauline tradition, John XXIII, 88

Petrine claims (Matt 16:13–19), 105

Petrine heritage: holy catholic church and, 117; shepherding etc., 117

Petrine primacy: 122; also *inter pares,* 135; in New Testament, 133, 135; theme of, 82

Petrine succession, doctrine of, 118

Petrine text, 117

Petrus, 75

Pharisaic teaching, 35

Philip, apostle, 66

Philip at Ephesus, presbyter, 148

Piazza di San Pietro: 103; statues in, 133

pillars, order of, 143; those "who seemed to be," 6

pillars of church, Paul's communion with, 86

Pius IX, 84

Pius X, 148

Pius XII, 84

Plutarch, *historesai* as "getting information" about persons and things, 32

Polycarp: 17, 66–68, 139; copies 1 Clement 5 in reference to Peter, 20; effective in uniting apostolic tradition in Asia with martyrological tradition from Rome, 19; experienced faith

and hope of church in Rome,
14; Ignatius wrote to church in
Rome while staying in Smyrna
with, 17; Irenaeus' teacher, 14;
received 1 Peter in good faith,
19; represented church in Asia,
17; saw endurance of Ignatius
as example of obedience to
martyrological example of
Jesus, and united with
experience of Philippian church
with martyrdom, 19; teacher of
Irenaeus and close episcopal
colleague of Ignatius, 19; visit
with Anicetus, 57; with
concordant witness of Peter
and Paul, 17
Polycrates, 66–68
pontifex maximus, term of
mockery, 78
pope: 2; actions of, 127–28; both
Peter and Paul as authorities
for, 4; collegial consensus and
personal initiative, 88;
governing through prayer of
Peter and Paul, 96; heir of Peter
and Paul, 88; infallibility and
supreme and universal
jurisdiction of, 109; infallibility
of, 110; loyal criticism of, 127;
Peter's teaching handed on by,
94; relation to Peter, 110;
supreme and universal
jurisdiction of, 110; teaching as
judging, 94–95; visible center of
unity, 116
Pope John, and Protestants, 116
popes: formulating Petrine tasks
in Pauline terms, 10;
intercession of Peter and Paul,
93; missionary to nations, 88;
successors of Peter and Paul, 86
Poschmann, B., 77, 144
post-tridentine Catholic exegesis,
misguided, 80

potentior principalitas: foundation
by and martyrdom of Peter and
Paul, 81; from foundation by
Peter, 61
power of forgiveness, church's, 78
power of keys: handed over to
church, 76; received by Peter,
77; to local church and bishop,
77
power to exclude, bishops of
Rome, 85
power to forgive, 76
praedicatio, preaching, 69
Praxeas, reproached by
Tertullian, 143
preaching of gospel, Paul
empowered by Lord, 8
preaching, Paul's reaching all
nations of world, 9
pre-Constantinian church,
doctrine of presence, 120
pre-Pauline tradition, "Christ
died for our sins according to
the scriptures" (1 Cor 15:3), 50
presbyters: and penitent, 78;
practice of, 67
presence: "active ministry of
apostles," 97; at grave or in
worshiping community, 92; of
apostles with college of bishops,
91; Peter and Paul and (other)
martyrs, 120; Peter and Paul in
church of Rome, 73
presence of apostles in bishops,
97
presence of kingdom, bishops'
shepherding and teaching
within, 96
presence of Peter and Paul:
church of Rome, 97, 119–20;
Council of Ephesus, 94
primacy: 107–8; bishop of Rome,
123, 127; Catholic dogma of
Petrine, 9; deemphasis of
Petrine, 115–16; heritage of

Peter and Paul, 118; jurisdictional for bishop of Rome, 113; Peter's (1 Cor 15:3–11), 111
primacy of bishop of Rome, 2
primacy of Peter, acknowledged by Paul according to Victorinus and Ambrosiaster, 32
primacy of Rome, 118–19
princeps, 141
principalitas, 141
principalitas/principalis, 59
principatus, Peter's primacy, 134
problem, Roman Catholic, 108
prominence of Rome, 4
prophets and apostles, power of forgiveness, 78
prophets of Montanism, power of forgiveness, 78
propter potentiorem principalitatem, 59
Protestant perspective: 2, 98; real presence in eucharist, 120
Protestants: 3, 10, 98; and action by bishop of Rome, 128; and church of Rome, 129; and Pope John, 116; authority of Rome, 125; bishop of Rome, 118; communion with church of Rome, 129; concerns of, 10; list of considerations for, 126; perception of pope, 116; primacy of bishop of Rome, 118; question of episcopal collegiality among, 136; unity (ecumenical), 120
Protestants and Roman Catholics, 10
Protestants, Roman Catholics, and Orthodox, 3

Raya, J., 149
reconciliation, church's power of, 77–78

redemption, universality of Christ's, 86
redemptive power, in innocent suffering, 16
reform movements, Benedictine, Cistercian, Franciscan, 88
regula: 13, 140; determined by harmony between Peter and Paul, 48
renewal, fact and task, 97
research: ecumenical, vii; historical and theological, 1
"resourcement," 3
resurrection appearances: Paul believed that appearance of Lord to him was of same order as to other apostles, 27; Paul's direct experience of risen Christ served as control for tradition of, 27; tradition in 1 Corinthians 15:3–7, 27
resurrection of Jesus, probably discussed by Paul with some Christians who had experienced resurrection appearances, 27
Reumann, J., 138
revealed truth, 3
revealing activity of Christ, not restricted to appearances, 55
revelation: elements of, 3; God's, 3; identical to Peter and Paul, 54; not source of Paul's tradition of Lord's supper, 27; same for Peter and Paul, 55, 68
revelation of Jesus Christ (Gal 1:11–12), 34
revelation to Peter and Paul, identity of, 55
Richardson, C. C., 140
Righetti, M., 149
right hand of fellowship: 112–13; meanings and importance of, 133
risen Christ: inseparable from earthly Jesus, 56; not Paul's

source of tradition of Lord's supper, 27; Paul's authority from, 86

risen Lord, appearances of, 6

risk-taking out of love, endemic to Christian faith from heart of Jesus, 36

rock: 8; Peter and Jesus, 75

"rock of scandal," Christ, 75

role of bishop of Rome, 11

Roman Catholic, 3, 130

Roman Catholic bishops, Vatican II, 125

Roman Catholic church: 2, 4, 104; self-identity of, 127

Roman Catholic conclusions, 2

Roman Catholic dogma: 2; bishop of Rome, 123; papal primacy, 127

Roman Catholic formulation, obstacle to reunion, 125

Roman Catholic monk, 133

Roman Catholic perspective, 98

Roman Catholic theology, 2–3

Roman Catholic tradition, summary of, 128

Roman Catholicism, debate and evolution on collegiality in, 136

Roman Catholics: 3, 127–28; and "limits" on pope's power, 127; and papal primacy, 127; and universal supreme jurisdiction, 126; Petrine succession, 116; (ecumenical) unity, 120

Roman church, prominence of, 83

Roman curia, loyal criticism of, 127

Roman empire: capital of, 105; heads of two apostolic missions brought low in capital city of, 102

Roman law, women as witnesses, 111

Roman liturgy, 90–91

Romans: letter by Ignatius, 17; letter by Paul, 7, 146

Rome (church): 9, 21, 141; bishop as heir to both Peter and Paul, 10; bishop as model for every bishop and missionary of Jesus Christ, 10; bishop of, 9; bishop to encourage, test, and coordinate all charisms in church, 10; bishop's job description in Petrine and Pauline terms, 10; bishops of, 4; bishops sensitive to charismatic movements, 10; church no less an heir to Paul than to Peter, 9; church of, 4–5, 10; Clement of, 4; "first see of Peter," 83; martyrdom emanating from Jerusalem, 14; missionary thrusts initiated by, 10; normativity of, 70; relationship to Oriental churches, 127; scriptural continuity with Jerusalem, 14–15

Rome (city): 13; "Babylon" underlining martyrological significance of, 8; bear witness at, 14; before his letter Paul never preached in, 101; capital city of the empire, 100; Christian community in, 13; city of, 4–5; designated by Babylon as power hostile to God, 8; evidence of unified apostolic witness in, 14; international center, 60; joint martyrdom of Peter and Paul in, 4; martyrdom of Peter and Paul in, 14; Paul's letter to God's beloved in, 101; locus for memorials to Peter and Paul's obedience unto death, 104; martyrdom of Peter and Paul in but not solely for, 104;

martyrological tradition in, 113–14; Paul in, 141; Paul's arrival and witnessing there as providential climax and consummation of his apostolic mission, 7; Paul's martyrdom in, 14; Paul's *martyresai* and martyrdom in, 7; Paul's mission concludes with preaching ministry in, 7–8; persecution in, 117; Peter and Paul martyred together in, 9; Peter to, 8; Polycarp brought faith of apostles as it was celebrated in Asia to, 17; represented as Babylon in 1 Peter, 14; visited by Polycarp, 17

Rome's special position, from Peter and Paul's joint activity, 62

Romulus and Remus: legendary twin founders of Rome, 103; not underlying Tertullian's comments on apostles' teaching and martyrdom (*Pre* 36.3), 103; Peter and Paul comparable "fathers" according to St. Leo the Great, 103

Rousseau, A., 58, 140

Rousseau and Doutreleau, 59, 61

rule of faith, "fourteenth day" related to, 67

sacred history, 11

sacrifice of Jesus, benefits of, 119

sacrificial death of Christ, chief model for faithful, 15

St. Leo the Great: bishop as successor of Peter, 83; Peter and Paul are "the fathers" of Rome comparable to Romulus and Remus, 103

St. Paul's-outside-the-Walls, prayer and worship at, 133–34

St. Peter's (cathedral): architecture says Christ and his disciple-apostles are exalted and are represented on streets by Peter and Paul, 103; Christ and twelve apostles lining top of facade, 103

St. Peter's Basilica, Peter's presence in Rome, 93

saints, communion of, 144

salvation history, Paul's martyrdom in context of, 14

San Sebastiano, graffiti on walls of, 92–93

Sapir, Baruch, 139

Satan: 8; instruments of, 125; Peter, 125; wiles of, 119

Schönmetzer, A., 147

scholarship, biblical, 6

scripture, 9

Schütz, Roger, Protestant prior of Taize, 88

Schwarts, E., 148

Scott, Robert, 139

scripture canon, 3

scriptures: 3; *regula* or canon of, 13; church's tradition an important key in understanding the, 3

second century: church of, 3; great church in, 3

second-century church: 4–5; judgment of, 3

Second Peter, implies that Peter holds key to right interpretation of Pauline corpus, 7

Second Timothy, 8

Second Vatican Council (1962–65): 135; by-product of, 132; closing service of, 133; *see* Vatican II

sedes, location of teaching, 94–95

Servant, sent into world, 119

servant of Lord, bishop of Rome, 118

shepherd, God the Father, 90–91
shepherding, not succession but participation and representation, 91
Sidon, 39
Simon (Magus), 142
Siricus, ministry of Peter, 93
"sister" church of Rome, 127
Slavic nations, missionary thrust to, 10, 88
Socrates, 142
Sodom, 40
Son of Man gives his life as a ransom for many (Matt 20:25–28; Mark 10:42–45), evidence of Isaiah 53, 50
Spain: mission to, 7; Paul will go to (Rom 15:23–24), 100
Spirit, inspired by, 67
statues of Peter and Paul: symbolism of, 133; twin founders of new Roman civilization, 103
stumbling block, 8
succession: original, 59; Petrine, 1, 116
succession of presbyter-bishops, 59–60
succession versus heritage, 85–86
suffering: Christ's linked with that of faithful, 16; power and glory of Christ in, 89; redemptive power of innocent, 16
suffering Christ, authority of, 24
sufferings of Christ, completed, 119
Sunday, Easter controversy, 65–66
"super-apostles" (2 Cor), 49
Sylvester, letter to, 83
Synod of Arles (314 A.D.), 4, 82, 149
synods, regional on Easter controversy, 66
synoptic gospels: authenticity of,

56; Peter as chief guarantor of tradition of Jesus and leader of twelve, 7
Syria, Christian mission into, 44
Syria and Cilicia, Paul's going "into Syria and Cilicia" a directional phrase, 29
systematic theology: martyrdom, 119–20; Roman Catholic, 98, 107

Talley, T. J., 142
Tertullian: 2, 4, 112, 142, 146, 148; agreement of Peter and Paul, 69; anti-Marcionite concern, 70; apostolic churches, 70; apostolic martyrdom and church-founding, 71; denounces Catholic church, 143; development by, 133; doctrine of participation, 81; favoring Peter, 69; first quotation of Matthew 16:18–19, 80; first use of Matthew 16:18–19, 75; goal of, 145; influence of Rome, 143; Peter and Paul "poured their whole teaching along with their blood" into church of Rome (*Pre* 36.3), 99–100; presence of Peter and Paul in church of Rome, 73; "primitive" traditions, 98; quasi-martyrdom of John, 81; recognized normative importance of apostolic conference, 48; Rome and John, 143; Romulus and Remus not behind writings about teaching and martyrdom of Peter and Paul (*Pre* 36.3), 103–4; shift relationship between Peter and Paul, 70; subordination of Paul to Peter, 80; three witnesses for founding, 72–73

The Centuries, 130
themelioo, church-founding by
  Peter and Paul, 61
themeliosantes, Pauline
  terminology, 61
theologians: in faculty seminar,
  132; Roman Catholic, 108
theological positions, Methodist
  and Roman Catholic, 2
theology: patristic, 9; Roman
  Catholic, 2-3; systematic, 9
Theophrastus, 139
third century, 4
Third World Conference of Faith
  and Order, Lund (1952), 131
thronos, location of teaching, 94-
  95
Tillard, J. M. R., 1, 138, 147
Tillich, Paul, 127
"to visit" or "to get to know,"
  Paul's meaning (Gal 1:18), 28
tois, dative of reference, not of
  agent, 61
tradition: biblical, liturgical, and
  patristic, 1; Christian, 9;
  church's as important key in
  understanding scriptures, 3;
  coming from apostles, 5;
  earliest patristic, 9; Paul took
  pains to be sure about, 27;
  patristic and liturgical, 3; Peter
  and Paul as founders, 107; pre-
  Pauline (1 Cor 15:3-11), 111;
  pro-Petrine (Matt 16:17-19),
  109-10; resurrection
  appearances, 27; Roman
  Catholic, 3
tradition concerning Lord's
  supper: Corinthian assurance
  from Paul that it originated
  with Jesus, 26; not to Paul by
  revelation from risen Christ,
  27
tradition of apostles, 141
tradition of resurrection

appearances, placed Peter and
  twelve at beginning, 27
traditions: 6; Petrine, 1
traditions of synoptic gospels and
  John, confirmation by Peter's
  apostolic authority, 86
truth, of apostolic faith, 11
Trantham, Henry, 139
triumphalism, taboo against,
  132
Troeltsch, origins of ecumenical
  church history, 131
truth: *histor* ascertained not
  philosophical kind but kind
  issuing in practical wisdom, 30;
  revealed, 3
"truth of gospel," 34
twofold apostolic mission to Jews
  and Gentiles, 107
Tyre, 39

union, organic, 134
united apostolic authority of
  Peter and Paul, 13
unity: conciliar or confederated,
  134; of Peter and Paul, 135; of
  Testaments and of God, 72;
  "organic," 134; spiritual, 134
unity in church, Holy Spirit as
  transcendent principle of, 92
unity-in-diversity, for survival,
  137
unity-in-*diversity,* only viable
  option, 137
unity of church: by Holy Spirit,
  97; pope's ministry of, 85
union of earthly and heavenly
  church, 97
universal church: 1, and popes,
  125-26; consultation with, 126;
  infallibility of, 2; Peter and
  Paul's mission for, 5; Peter as
  foundation for, 74; role of
  bishop of Rome, 123; unity of,
  126-27

Valentinians: 140; deny prophecy, 54

Valentinus, 142

Vardaman, E. Jerry, 139

Vatican I: 147, 150; definition of infallibility and universal jurisdication, 109; Peter as center of unity, 85

Vatican II: 3, 10, 99, 125; called by John XXIII, 88; development after, 127; Petrine primacy in, 115–16

Vatican Council of 1870, 107. *See* Vatican I

Vatican decrees of 1870, 110–11

versions of New Testament, Latin, Coptic and Syriac, 31

vetus traditio, true tradition, 60

Victor: 65–68, 142; attitude opposed by Irenaeus, 68; bishop with power to exclude, 85, 115; exclusion and martyrdom, 115

Victorinus, Paul's visit an acknowledgment of "the primacy of Peter," 32

Vinck, J. de, 149

virginal conception, support by Peter's confession, 55–56

visit: Paul and Peter in Jerusalem for fifteen days, 28; Peter by Paul, 6

von Ranke, origins of ecumenical church history, 131

western church, missionary thrust of, 88

westward mission to Gentiles, Paul laid groundwork in three-year interval, 29–30

whole people of God, preservation by, 127

widows, and church order, 76

Williamson, G. A., 144

witness: apostolic, 3–4; apostolic of holy catholic faith, 17; as martyr, 5

witness of Peter and Paul, 134

witness of Peter and Paul, living word of God, 129

witnessing, joint, 5

witnessing to Christ, 5

worship, and presence of martyrs, 120

Xystus: Peter in Pauline terms, 94; Peter's presence in Rome, 93; pope actualizes apostolic teaching, 94

Zebulun, land of, 42

Zizioulas, J. D., 150

INDEX OF TEXTS

References of quotations of one sentence or more have page numbers italicized.

OLD TESTAMENT

Deuteronomy		Daniel	
19:15	5, *72*	3:6	15
Psalms		Hosea	
22	*23*	6:2	45
Isaiah		Jonah	
8:14	75	2:1	45
9:1–2	*42*		
53	6, *22–23*, 24, 45, 50		

NEW TESTAMENT

Matthew		19:28	95
4:13–14	42	20:25–26	*21*
10:16–22	104	20:25–28	50
10:16–23	*102–3*	20:26b–28	*21–22*
11:21–24	*39–40*	24:9–14	*104*
11:25–27	54–55	24:14	*104–5*
16	145	26:17–30	50
16:13–19	105, 107, 116	28:1–10	111
16:17	54–55	28:19	40
16:17–18	61	28:20	*104*
16:17–19	8, 61–62, *109–10,* 141		
16:18–19	68, 74–75, 80–81, 83, 141, 145	Mark	
16:21–24	8	8:33	*109*
18:16	5	10:42–45	50
18:18	81	10:43b–45	*21–22*

Luke		15:30–33	*100–1*
9:28	143	15:32	101, *104*
11:52	76		
		1 Corinthians	
John		1:10–12	23
8:19	5	1:10–13	*24*
8:44	19	1:12	*48–49*
12:31	*150*	1:17–18	*24*
13:23	74	3:10–11	75
13:25–26	74	3:11	81
14	55	4:9–16	*24–25*
19:26–27	75	4:17	*25*
21:15–19	8	5:4	128
21:18–19	8	6	128
		7	128
Acts		7:22	17
1:15–26	110	7:23	18
		9:1	34
Acts		9:19–22	69
10	148	10–11	128
10:1–11:18	122	10:4	75, 81
15	135	10:16–17	*26*
20:6	37	11:1	*26*
20:18–38	7	11:23–26	6, *26*, 39
21:4	37	12:3	4
21:7	37	13:10–11	61
21:8	66	15:1–7	6
23:11	8, 14	15:3	*50*, 94
25:13–14	37	15:3–6	110–11
28:14	37	15:3–7	27, *45*
		15:6	27
		15:8	34
Romans		15:8–9	19
1:1–6	101	15:8–11	*46*
1:7a	*100*	15:58	20
1:8	142	16:22	4
1:8b	*100*		
1:13	*100*	**2 Corinthians**	
8:17	20	5:15	20
15:5	101	11:28	*88*
15:5–6	*100*	13:1	5
15:20	61		
15:22	*100*	**Galatians**	
15:23–24	*100*	1:1	*33*, 54
15:28b–29	*100*	1–2	69

1:8–9	4
1:11–12	32, *33–34*
1:12	34, 54–55
1:15	34
1:16	28, 54–55
1:17	28–29, 33
1:18	6, 28, 30, 48, 139
1:18–24	122
1:20	27
1:21	28–29
1:22	28
1:23	28, 45
1:24	28
2	80, 135
2:1–10	6, 29, 48, 124
2:2	20
2:5	27
2:7–9	*47–48*
2:9	9, 133, 143
2:11–14	*128*
2:11–21	48
2:14	27

Ephesians

2:20	61

Philippians

2:16	20

Colossians

1:23	20

1 Thessalonians

5:10	20

1 Timothy

2:7	84
3:1–13	76
5:9–10	76
5:19	5

2 Timothy

4:6	8
4:10	20
4:16	20
4:16–18	8
4:17	9

1 Peter

1:7	8, *15*
1:18–19	*15*, 18
2:21–25	*15*
2:22	19
2:24	19
3:16–19	*16*
3:18	55
4:1–2	16
4:12	8
4:12–15	*16*
4:16	19
5:3	124
5:8–11	*17*
5:9	20
5:13	8, *17*

2 Peter

2	135
3:15	7

1 John

3:8	19
4:2–4	19
4:9	19

Revelation

14:8	8
16:9	8
17:5	8
18:2	8

NON-CANONICAL CHRISTIAN TEXTS

Ambrose
Faith
4.5.57   146
Expositions in Luke
6.97–98   146
Epistles
43.9   146

Augustine
Retractions
1.21   146

Clement of Rome
Epistle to the Corinthians
5   20–21
5.4–7   140
16   22

Cyprian
Epistles
20–26   145

Eusebius of Caesarea
Ecclesiastical History
2.25.8   140
5.1.41   62–63
5.2.5   144
5.22.2–3   66
5.23.3–4   67
5.23.6   66
5.24.2   66
5.24.6   66
5.24.8   67
5.24.12–13   66
5.24.16–17   67–68
5.42.5   144
Life of Constantine
3.14–24   142

Gregory I
Letter to Eulogius
  Alexandrinus   150

Hilary of Poitiers
On the Trinity
2.23   146
6.20   146
6.36–37   146

Ignatius
To the Ephesians
10   20
To the Romans
2.1   63, 148
3.2–3   63
4   17
4–5   18
4.3   5, 63, 140
6   18, 20
9   18

Irenaeus
Against Heresies
1.11.1   65
1.13.6   54
1.13.16   140
1.16.3   54
1.26.1   141
1.31.1   141
2.13.1   141
2.17.3   141
3   140
3.2.8   141
3.3.2   5, 48, 138, 140
3.3.2–3   13, 57–58
3.3.3   4, 51
3.4.1   142
3.4.2   142
3.4.3   142
3.12.13   62
3.12.15   54
3.13.1   54, 74
3.13.2   54
3.15.1–3   55
3.15.3   141

3.16.6	141
3.21.3	*142*
4.20.2	141
4.26.2	141, *142*
4.33.8–9	62
4.35.2	*54,* 141
4.38.3	141
5.14.1–2	141
5.21.1	141
5.28.40	63

Jerome
Against Jovian

1.26	146
2.37	146

Commentary on Matthew

16.18	146

Epistles

15.2	146

John Chrysostom
Commentary on Galatians

1.1	146

Homilies on Matthew

54.3	146
82.3	146

Leo the Great
*Sermon 82, On the
    Feastday of Peter and
    Paul* 147, 150

Nicholas I
Epistles

86	147

Origen
Catenae Fragmentae

345.11	146

Commentary on Matthew

12.11–14	146

Homilies in Exodus

5.4	146

Polycarp of Smyrna
Letter to the Philippians

7–8	*19*
9–10	*19–20*

Socrates
Ecclesiastical History

1.8–9	142

Tertullian
Against Marcion

1.20.2–3	69–70
3.9.4	72
4.2.1–5	140
4.2.5	*143*
4.3.3	69–70, 143
4.13.6	*75,* 145
4.22.7	72
5.3.6	143
5.3.6–8	70
5.12.9	72

Antidote (against the Scorpion's
Sting)

7.4	71
10.8	76–77, *79,* 145
15.3	*73*

Apology

21.25	71–72
50.13	72
50.14–16	72

Baptism

6.2	72

Chastity

7.2–3	76
13.4	76

Modesty

21.5–10	145
21.7	*78*
21.9	76
21.9–10	*78–79,* 145
21.11	76
21.11–15	145
21.12	76

21.16–17	*78*	
22.1	143	
22.9–11	77	
Monogamy		
8.4	*76*, 145	
11.4	76	
Penitence		
8.4–6	*78*	
Praxeas		
1.5	*143*, 148	
Prayer		
20.2	*142*	

Prescription (for Heretics)	
22.4–5	*74*
22.6	72
23.1	69
23.9	69
23.10	69
36.1	71
36.1–2	70–71, 73
36.3	71–73, *103–4, 112, 146*
To Martyrs	
1.6	77

THEOLOGICAL INQUIRIES:

Serious studies on contemporary questions of Scripture, Systematics and Moral Theology. Also in the series:

J. Louis Martyn, *The Gospel of John in Christian History: Essays for Interpreters*

Frans Jozef van Beeck, S.J., *Christ Proclaimed: Christology as Rhetoric*

John P. Meier, *The Vision of Matthew: Christ, Church and Morality in the First Gospel*

Pheme Perkins, *The Gnostic Dialogue: The Early Church and the Crisis of Gnosticism*

Michael L. Cook, S.J., *The Jesus of Faith: A Study in Christology*

Joseph F. Wimmer, *Fasting in the New Testament: A Study in Biblical Theology*

William R. Farmer and Denis M. Farkasfalvy, O.Cist., *The Formation of the New Testament Canon: An Ecumenical Approach*

Rosemary Rader, *Breaking Boundaries: Male/Female Friendship in Early Christian Communities*

Richard J. Clifford, *Fair Spoken and Persuading: An Interpretation of Second Isaiah*

Robert J. Karris, *Luke: Artist and Theologian: Luke's Passion Account as Literature*

Jerome Neyrey, S.J., *The Passion According to Luke: A Redaction Study of Luke's Soteriology*

Frank J. Matera, *Passion Narratives and Gospel Theologies: Interpreting the Synoptics through their Passion Stories*

James P. Hanigan, *Homosexuality: The Test Case for Christian Sexual Ethics*

Robert A. Krieg, *Story-Shaped Christology: The Role of Narratives in Identifying Jesus Christ*

Brad H. Young, *Jesus and His Jewish Parables: Rediscovering the Roots of Jesus' Teaching*

Dimitri Z. Zaharopoulous, *Theodore of Mopsuestia on the Bible: A Study of His Old Testament Exegesis*